Consumer Collective Redress in EU Law

This book provides critical insights into the framework of consumer collective redress within EU law, including recent changes introduced by the Representative Actions Directive (EU) 2020/1828. The focus is on Poland, where group proceedings have been operating since 2009. The exploration of Poland's 15-year time-span experience constitutes a comprehensive case study, offering valuable examples and recommendations.

The study examines whether, collective redress mechanisms can ensure effective enforcement of consumer rights and, at the same time, guarantee a high level of consumer protection. The discussion is composed of three fundamental parts. The first chapter explores the nature of collective redress from the perspective of EU law. In the second chapter, the book addresses the various legal mechanisms operating in the Member States and the UK that serve consumers as means of collective redress. The final chapter focuses on Poland, discussing the legislative framework and functioning of group proceedings in practice. The discussion is enriched with specific solutions for the further development of collective redress in the EU.

This book covers issues that will be of interest to researchers investigating EU consumer law, collective redress, class actions and law enforcement more in general. It will be of relevance to consumers and practitioners, including attorneys and consumer organisations aiming to bring representative actions in one of the EU Member States.

Jagna Mucha, PhD, is an Assistant Professor at the Chair of Transnational Law, Faculty of Law and Administration of the University of Warsaw, Poland. Her academic interests revolve around EU and transnational law, different methods of consumer law enforcement and the problem of access to justice. She conducted several studies in this field, among others, at the Harvard Law School, the University of Oxford and Ludwig-Maximilians University in Munich. She is a grant holder of the scholarships of Foundation for Polish Science (*Fundacja na rzecz Nauki Polskiej*), German Academic Exchange Service (*Deuscher Akademischer Austauschdienst*), Kościuszko Foundation and Polish National Science Centre (*Narodowe Centrum Nauki*).

Routledge Research in EU Law

Delegation of Powers in the EU Legal System
Annalisa Volpato

The Tangled Complexity of the EU Constitutional Process
The Frustrating Knot of Europe
Giuseppe Martinico

Instruments of Public Law
Digital Transformation during the Pandemic
Irena Lipowicz, Grażyna Szpor and Aleksandra Syryt

The European Union as a Normative Power
The Role of the CJEU
Yuval Reinfeld

Implementing International Disability Law in the European Union
A Substantive and Procedural Appraisal
Ottavio Quirico

Cybersecurity and EU Law
Adopting the Network and Information Security Directive
Theodoros Karathanasis

Consumer Collective Redress in EU Law
Lessons from the Polish Legal System
Jagna Mucha

https://www.routledge.com/Routledge-Research-in-EU-Law/book-series/ROUTEULAW

Consumer Collective Redress in EU Law

Lessons from the Polish Legal System

Jagna Mucha

Routledge
Taylor & Francis Group
LONDON AND NEW YORK

First published 2026
by Routledge
4 Park Square, Milton Park, Abingdon, Oxon OX14 4RN

and by Routledge
605 Third Avenue, New York, NY 10158

Routledge is an imprint of the Taylor & Francis Group, an informa business

British Library Cataloguing-in-Publication Data
A catalogue record for this book is available from the British Library

ISBN: 978-1-032-85493-9 (hbk)
ISBN: 978-1-032-86003-9 (pbk)
ISBN: 978-1-003-52084-9 (ebk)

DOI: 10.4324/9781003520849

Typeset in Times New Roman
by Deanta Global Publishing Services, Chennai, India

Mojej Mamie

Contents

Acknowledgements *viii*

Introduction 1

1 Consumer collective redress in EU law 8

1.1 Terminological remarks 9

1.2 EU collective redress vs. US class action mechanism 10

1.3 Different routes to the EU consumer collective redress framework 15

1.4 Challenges to consumer law enforcement under Directive 2009/22/EC 18

1.5 Addressing the problems in the Proposal for RAD 24

1.6 A critical review of the collective redress framework within RAD 34

1.7 Conclusion 41

2 Private enforcement of consumer collective interests: A comparative perspective 47

2.1 Belgium 48

2.2 The Netherlands 57

2.3 England and Wales 69

2.4 Conclusion 73

3 Pursuing consumer collective claims in group proceedings in Poland 80

3.1 Legislative framework for consumer collective redress in Poland 81

3.2 Data and analysis 85

3.3 Group proceedings before the District Court in Warsaw 88

3.4 Institutional support for consumers in group proceedings 98

3.5 Implementation of RAD in Poland 105

3.6 Conclusion 112

Annex no. 1: List of case files for group proceedings pending and/or closed between 01.01.2013-30.06.2020 before the District Court in Warsaw *121*

Index *124*

Acknowledgements

This volume summarises the findings of the research project funded by the Polish National Science Centre (NCN), ‘Consumer collective redress in the group proceedings in the Polish legal system in the light of the European Union law standards—achievements and challenges,’ no. 2018/28/C/HS5/00083, grant Sonatina 2.

The University of Warsaw generously established open access.

I would like to warmly thank all my friends in academia and legal practice for their advice and critical comments on the initial version of this book.

Introduction

Collective redress remains a highly controversial concept in the EU in respect of the need for its introduction and design. Its final shape, based on the procedural mechanism of representative action, was achieved in 2020 as a result of the political consensus reached by the Member States. After decades of discussions and hesitation, many issues were still too controversial to regulate at the EU level. Therefore, Directive 2020/1828 on Representative Actions (RAD)[1] leaves significant discretion regarding its implementation in the Member States. Thus, it is not surprising that the new instrument is far from perfect. A lot has already been said in this respect in the legal discourse. Still, one general conclusion can be reached from this discussion—the success of effective collective redress depends entirely on the Member States and their enforcement procedures. With this in mind, the national perspectives are vital to solve the puzzle of effective consumer collective redress.

This book, having an evidence-based character, attempts to examine the system of consumer collective redress in Poland. Interestingly, this mechanism has been operating there since 2009, when the law on group proceedings was introduced. One can assume that with almost 15 years of operation, Poland has sufficient experience so far, which enables us to reflect on the functioning of the law. However, although the number of group actions submitted to the courts seems promising, only a few cases reached the final phase of proceedings in which the court decided on merits.

The study aims to investigate whether representative actions serve as a mechanism that facilitates the effective enforcement of consumer rights within the European Union. The primary objective is to verify the hypothesis that, through an in-depth analysis of Poland as a case study, a collective redress mechanism significantly contributes to ensuring a high level of consumer protection. The research in this field is justified due to the process of globalisation of consumer markets, which means many consumers are likely

1 Directive (EU) 2020/1828 of the European Parliament and of the Council of 25 November 2020 on representative actions for the protection of the collective interests of consumers and repealing Directive 2009/22/EC, OJEU of 4.12.2020 No. L 409 p. 1.

DOI: 10.4324/9781003520849-1

to be affected by the same or similar practices of a given trader. Even though the damage caused by such a trader for individual consumers usually involves small amounts, the mass claim submitted by a large group of consumers or their representatives may be significant to the market. Therefore, infringements of consumer rights that affect a vast number of individuals may distort markets, making it challenging to deliver an innovative and competitive consumer-oriented economy.[2]

How can collective redress influence the level of consumer protection, and what does it involve? In simple terms, it expands the conventional view of civil proceedings, putting multiple individual claims the central focus by creating the possibility of obtaining redress for the group.[3] It allows, for procedural economy and efficiency of enforcement, many similar legal claims to be bundled into a single court action. Collective redress facilitates access to justice in particular cases where the individual damage is so low that potential claimants would not think it is worth pursuing an individual claim. It also strengthens the negotiating power of potential claimants and contributes to the efficient administration of justice by avoiding many individual proceedings concerning claims resulting from the same infringement of law.[4]

On the other hand, it seems evident that traders are not interested in introducing collective redress since it always involves additional costs of proceedings. When there is no effective mechanism for law enforcement in place, traders benefit from the rational apathy of consumers unwilling to pursue claims in courts. The main argument voiced over the years by the business environment against the class action system is that, at least in theory, it entails the risk of abusive and frivolous litigation. Hence, in the process of designing the system of collective redress, it is indispensable to strike a balance and find measures that would enable the enforcement of consumer rights and, at the same time, guarantee the safeguards for traders.

Despite the EU institutions' awareness that effective procedural mechanisms can significantly enhance consumer protection, they have primarily concentrated on substantive law so far. The EU consumer policy aims to balance the market position of consumers and traders. This was expressed, on the one hand, by undertaking initiatives consisting of imposing extensive information-related duties on the professionals and, on the other hand, by avoiding the scenario of the weaker party being insufficiently informed, equipping consumers with new rights, among others, the right to withdraw from the contract, (leading to restricting the principle *pacta sunt servanta*), prohibition of some behaviours, that is protection against unfair, abusive contractual clauses or guarantees of minimal rights that cannot be contractually waived. Until recently, collective

2 Green Paper of the European Commission dated 27.11.2008 on consumer collective redress, COM(2008) 794 final version.

3 Wrbka, van Uytsel, Siems (2012).

4 Communication from the Commission to the European Parliament, the Council, the European Economic and Social Committee and the Committee of the Regions, Towards a European Horizontal Framework for Collective Redress, COM(2013) 401 final version.

redress, being a procedural mechanism, has not become a widely discussed form of enforcing the law and has not attracted enough attention in public debate or the literature on the subject. In comparison to the first solution outlined in the substantive law regulations, which were introduced at the early stage of development of the European Union, it was noticed comparatively late that consumer protection remains ephemeral if it is not supplemented by a mechanism to execute the rights granted effectively or if this process is made difficult, given, for example, the necessity to cover high costs or long waiting time for the judgement. This is why the EU started to make up for the missing legislation in the field of procedural solutions, mainly through the introduction of solutions aiming to facilitate seeking redress in individual proceedings (with the leading example of European small claims procedure) or legislation on alternative consumer dispute resolution methods (ADR Directive).

The idea of collective redress in the EU was controversial from the outset. To some extent only, it was first regulated as a hard law in Directive 98/27/EC on injunctions for the protection of consumers' interests.[5] The main shortcoming of this act was that it did not allow consumers who suffered from infringement of the EU law to claim damages. Besides its deterrent effect, injunction decision brought no benefit to consumers. They could not have joined the injunciton proceeding and claim compensation but, instead, they were obliged to initiate additional separate follow-up actions (individual or collective) against the trader.

The problem of the limited effect of injunctions has been noticed by the Court of Justice of the European Union (CJEU). In case C-472/10 *Invitel*, the CJEU adjudicated that where the national court has recognised the unfair nature of a term included in the consumer contracts in an action for an injunction, such action affects all consumers who concluded an agreement with the same terms, including also those consumers who were not a party to the injunction proceedings.[6] This line of reasoning was developed further by the latter case C-119/15 *Partner*.[7] The CJEU specified there that it is for the national court to verify that the trader has an effective judicial remedy against the decision on the injunction. Recently, in the famous-319/20 *Meta* judgment, it has been confirmed that consumer organisations may bring opt-out representative actions against traders infringing data protection rights if national law permits so.[8]

5 Directive 98/27/EC of the European Parliament and of the Council of 19 May 1998 on injunctions for the protection of consumers' interests, OJEU of 11.6.1998, No L 166 p. 51, repealed by Directive 2009/22/EC of the European Parliament and of the Council of 23 April 2009 on injunctions for the protection of consumers' interest, OJEU of 1.5.2009 No L 110 p. 30.

6 Judgment of the CJEU of 26.04.2012, case C-472/10 *Nemzeti Fogyasztóvédelmi Hatóság v. Invitel Távközlési Zrt*, ECLI:EU:C:2012:242, para 44.

7 Judgment of the CJEU of 21.12.2016 in case C-119/15 *Biuro podróży "Partner" sp. z o.o. sp. k. v. Prezes UOKiK*, ECLI:EU:C:2016:987, para 47.

8 Judgment of the CJEU of 28.04.2022 in case C-318/20 *Meta Platforms Ireland Limited v. Bundesverband der Verbraucherzentralen und Verbraucherverbände – Verbraucherzentrale Bundesverband e.V.*, ECLI:EU:C:2022:322, para 83.

Undoubtedly, implementing measures to protect the collective interests of consumers is a challenging endeavour for the legislator.[9] For example, there are some explicit limitations arising from the specific functioning of the collective entities, such as: (i) the necessity to create a certain group of people who want to seek redress in legal proceedings and who are willing to bear the costs of the proceedings, (ii) organisational barriers arising out of different places of residence or seat of entities potentially interested in the participation in the court proceedings, (iii) distributing information about the mass claim to all the potentially interested claimants, and (iv) the necessity to agree upon the standard strategy, encompassing, for example, the disputed amount, which—in principle—should be equal for all the participants. On top of this are the business concerns regarding the risk of abusive and frivolous litigation, which also needs to be addressed in the legislative framework.

The limitations mentioned earlier led me to consider the structure that the EU collective redress system should effectively adopt. To achieve this goal, it was helpful to analyze the strategies used to address these challenges at the national level. After scrutinising the model of the collective redress proposed at the EU level, this book examines different legal mechanisms enabling to claim redress as a group in different EU Member States and in the UK. These mechanisms are based in particular on collective actions (complaints) which—depending on the solutions adopted in the legal system—may cover either group of people defined in abstract terms, for example, by pointing to their common feature, or specific persons who expressed explicit consent to participate in the group.[10] Thus, the aim is to identify tools and strategies related to collective consumer redress at the national level and examine whether and how they could fit in and complement the EU legal system. Because the collective litigation is rooted in the common law system, the study refers to British law and the US class action system.

Since analyzing EU law requires a deep connection to the domestic legal system, the research question is focused on how EU solutions translate into Polish law. Exploring such interdependence involves the examination of the relevant EU legal sources and legal acts passed by the Polish legislator and drawing adequate consolations. For this goal, the study aims to analyze and assess the Polish Act on Pursuing Claims in Group Proceedings of 17 December 2009 with the latest amendments.[11] In the horizontal perspective, the primary concern should be to discuss whether the above-mentioned act of Polish law can be viewed through the prism of the common law class action system, or—in reverse—through the prism of the mechanisms found in the legal systems of other EU Member States. From the vertical perspective, the

9 Kramer (2013).

10 Stier, Tzankova (2016).

11 In Polish: ustawa z dnia 17 grudnia 2009 o dochodzeniu roszczeń w postępowaniu grupowym, Dz.U. 2010 nr 7, poz. 44 (ze zmianami).

goal of the book is to examine said act as to its compliance with EU law and to verify whether the national legislator undertook to provide the high level of consumer protection, as stipulated by the Directive 2020/1828 on Representative Actions ('RAD').

Furthermore, this book aims to assess the effectiveness of the Polish system of consumer collective redress, encompassing primarily such factors as admissibility of collective redress, legal standing of the parties, funding of collective actions, or duration of the proceedings. However, analyzing only the legislative framework and the 'law in books' will not be enough to evaluate the state of consumer collective redress in Poland. Therefore, the research aims to investigate Polish case law regarding group proceedings in civil cases initiated before the competent Polish district courts (in Polish: *sądy okręgowe*)

In that way, the study outlines the factual and current status quo, tools and mechanisms that facilitate collective redress in Poland, as well as its evaluation, and it recommends changes to enhance effectiveness, coordination and synergy. The book's findings create a complex program analysis concerning the state of collective redress in Poland, which includes the EU concept and the experiences of other Member States and the UK. An in-depth analysis of the Polish legal system constitutes a comprehensive source of knowledge about the advantages and risks associated with consumer collective redress. Still, it indicates which aspects are critical from the perspective of consumers' current needs.

The discussion in this book is composed of three fundamental parts.

The first chapter concerns the study of the nature of the concept of collective redress from the perspective of EU law. The term 'collective redress' was coined in opposition to the US-style class action system, which EU institutions have widely criticised. Therefore, after a brief introduction of key terminology, this chapter starts with a comparison of the EU collective redress mechanism and US-style class action. Further, it discusses the long and bumpy route to the legislative framework for collective consumer redress in the EU, starting from the first injunctive measures introduced in the late nineties and ending with Directive 2020/1828 on Representative Actions. The answers to the questions posed in this part enable me to move forward to the second and third analytical parts of the research, in which concrete findings implementing the concept of collective redress at the national level are presented.

The second chapter problematises various legal mechanisms that function in the Member States and in the UK serving the consumers as a means of collective redress. The primary analysis focuses on the legal solutions adopted in Belgium, the Netherlands and the UK, where collective redress mechanisms are fairly well-established. It includes the recent changes introduced to the national laws by the implementation of RAD.[12] The goal of this chapter is to indicate how these mechanisms operate in practice and which solutions are

12 Since the UK left the EU, the UK legal system obviously does not need to implement EU directives anymore and RAD is no exception here.

worth reception in other jurisdictions, including Poland, by the way of good practices.

The third chapter has a national dimension in that it attempts to assess the influence of the concept of collective redress on consumer law enforcement in Poland. In this chapter, I present the data and analysis of case studies of collective claims brought before district courts (in the first instance) in civil cases between 2013 and 2020. The Ministry of Justice provides statistical information, which shows that between 2010 and the end of June 2021, 319 collective actions were brought in civil cases before the all district courts in Poland.This statistical information does not refer to any particular court file numbers or any specific regional courts, and therefore, examination of this data serves only as a starting point before the in-depth analysis of group proceedings, pending before the District Court in Warsaw (in Polish: *Sąd Okręgowy w Warszawie*). The analysis of court files is further complemented by observations of different institutions and stakeholders involved with group proceedings: municipal (regional) consumer ombudsmen (in Polish: *miejscy/ powiatowi rzecznicy konsumentów)* submitting group actions, representatives of the Financial Ombudsman (in Polish: *Rzecznik Finansowy*), the Polish Commissioner for Human Rights (in Polish *Rzecznik Praw Obywatelskich*), the President of the Office of Competition and Consumer Protection (in Polish: *Prezes UOKiK*) and some leading attorneys representing parties in group proceedings in Poland. The findings included in this part of the research cover also recent legislative changes introduced to the Polish law by implementation of RAD and the challenges and opportunities of this (not entirely) new model of representative actions. Based on such a research material, the third chapter of the book identifies and discusses the potential dysfunctions of the collective redress mechanism. To conclude, it provides some concrete solutions to the challenges identified above.

The findings presented in this book are based, first of all, on the dogmatic method. However, it needs to be added that Zygmunt Ziembiński claimed that legal dogma

> is to serve the purpose of proposing a solution that would enable [us] to retrieve a norm which effectively works towards materializing intended effects in the social life and this being done on the grounds of a specific concept of the sources of law which – in many respects – shows freedom as to the solution about a given norm being binding in a specific system'.[13]

Hence, to understand the expected influence of the EU law on the actual situation of consumers, it was indispensable to carry out an analysis of the empirical material that covers the data related to the collective complaints in the civil cases lodged at the district courts in Poland and conduct a study of the reasons for

13 Ziembiński (1980).

which some of them were rejected, denied, or returned to the consumers. The fact remains that only based on the analysis of the real needs of the consumers can we determine the expected model of collective consumer redress and subsequently confront it with the legislative initiatives undertaken. Apart from the dogmatic approach, the research used the analytical method. The comparative method was used to identify the solutions emerging from good practices found in the legal systems of Member States that are worth being adopted in Polish law. The conclusions formulated are also based on the interpretation of the normative material, the analysis of the input of international scholars, and the jurisdiction of the Court of Justice of the EU and Polish courts that is relevant here.

These findings concern one of the most significant problems: the functioning of the justice system in practice and theory. They are formulated in reaction to the discussion that was started a decade ago and concerns the future of integration processes facing globalisation and digitalisation challenges. One such challenge is to create a mechanism enabling one to react to consumer law infringments at the global dimension, which affect a vast number of individuals across many Member States. Effective enforcement mechanisms of collective redress are claimed to be the vital instrument facilitating access to justice. The issue of the justice system's effectiveness does not leave the agenda of meetings between EU institutions and Member States. Thus, it is surprising that despite its positive influence on facilitating access to justice, the concept of collective redress has neither been broadly discussed nor given its due place in the public debate or scholarly debate in Poland.

I hope that this book will trigger a discussion on the concept of collective redress in Poland. Regarding the socio-legal aspect of the research, it shall influence consumers by making them aware of collective redress mechanisms, especially regarding compensatory measures, and therefore increase society's trust in the justice system. This aspect, in turn, seems decisive for the social development of the individual Member States, including Poland, and for building civil society. However, if the collective redress mechanisms turn out to be ineffective, their use by consumers will not be beneficial, which will also bring some reflections.

References

Kramer X (2013) Enforcing mass settlements in the European Judicial Area: EU policy and the strange case of Dutch collective settlements, In: Hodges C, Stadler A (eds), *Resolving mass disputes. ADR and settlement of mass claims*, Edward Elgar.

Stier B, Tzankova I (2016) The culture of collective litigation: A comparative analysis, In: Hensler D, Hodges C, Tzankova I (eds), *Class actions in context: How culture, economics and politics shape collective litigation*, Edward Elgar Publishing.

Wrbka S, van Uytsel S, Siems M (2012) *Collective actions. Enhancing access to justice and reconciling multilayer interests?* Cambridge University Press.

Ziembiński Z (1980) *Problemy podstawowe prawoznawstwa*, Państwowe Wydawnictwo Naukowe.

1 Consumer collective redress in EU law

Consumer disputes are often characterised by a relatively small value of claim. Anywhere in the world, in cases that involve limited individual recovery, it is not economically feasible for consumers or for their lawyers to advance a claim for redress. This point is driven home by the oft-quoted remark by American Judge Posner that 'only a lunatic or a fanatic sues for \$30.'[1] However, if many small claims are aggregated into a single lawsuit, people are more likely to pursue their claims and lawyers are more willing to represent them before courts. In reality, collective redress might be the only mechanism that ameliorates the problem of small claims.

The described problem and the potential solution are not novel. However, until recently, the term 'collective redress' has not been widely part of the public debate in the EU. Nonetheless, European consumers are aware of the class action system that exists in the United States. This awareness is largely derived from the exposure of EU consumers to pervasive American cinematography, with probably the best-known example of the *Erin Brockovich* case, portrayed by Julia Roberts, and some news stories on class actions. While in the US the class action mechanism was first used some 50 years ago,[2] it was of limited use in litigation in the national courts of particular EU Member States. Although there is no single legal definition of collective redress, it seems to be generally accepted by scholars and policy makers that collective redress is an umbrella term that covers a wide range of procedural mechanisms tailored for the collective enforcement of consumer law. In spite of the fact that these mechanisms are very diverse—collective redress models and types differ significantly worldwide—they serve the same purpose: enabling many claimants to seek redress within a single proceeding.[3]

In this chapter, serving as a background for further discussion on the collective redress systems in particular jurisdictions, very brief terminological remarks are presented (1.1). In the opinion of the author, it is not possible

1 *Carnegie v. Household International*, 376 F.3rd at 656 (2004).
2 Rule 23, Federal Rules of Civil Procedure was adopted in 1966.
3 Amaro et al (2018: 13–14).

DOI: 10.4324/9781003520849-2

to examine the concept of collective redress without a short reference to the American class action system. Thus, the EU's and the US's approaches are compared to highlight the distinctions between these two concepts (1.2). Further, this chapter examines the long and bumpy route to establishing a legislative framework for collective consumer redress in the EU, starting from the critical assessment of the first injunctive measures introduced in late 1990s (1.3), with a focus on challenges with consumer law enforcement under Directive 2009/22/EC (1.4), followed by an examination of the controversial Proposal for the Representative Actions Directive (Proposal for RAD),[4] (1.5) and ending with an evaluation of the existing framework introduced by the final version of the Representative Actions Directive.[5] (1.6).

1.1 Terminological remarks

Due to the diversity of national collective redress systems, there is no coherent approach or universal definition of collective redress. However, there appears to be a consensus among scholars that the major forms of collective redress refer to court-based mechanisms initiated by private entities or individual victims. In the literature these mechanisms are also recognised under the umbrella term of 'mass litigation.'[6]

With respect to private enforcement, Micklitz and Durovic classify four major forms of collective redress: (i) the representative action, in which standing to bring an action on behalf of the group in order to get redress is granted to a representative entity; (ii) the group action, in which the aforementioned legal standing is granted to a member of the group; (iii) the model or test case, in which the action is initiated by one or more persons and in which the adopted judgment establishes the grounds for other cases brought against the same defendant; and (iv) the United States class action style, which is a form of group action led by professional lawyers who receive fees for their services and claim compensation for the clients.[7]

Different classification, which also refers to private enforcement, is proposed by Stoehr, who, as major forms of collective redress enumerates (i) group actions (including the US-style class action), (ii) representative actions,

4 Proposal for a Directive of the European Parliament and of the Council of 11.4.2018 on representative actions for the protection of the collective interests of consumers, and repealing Directive 2009/22/EC, COM/2018/0184 final – 2018/089 (COD), hereinafter referred to as "Proposal for RAD".

5 Directive (EU) 2020/1828 of the European Parliament and of the Council of 25 November 2020 on representative actions for the protection of the collective interests of consumers and repealing Directive 2009/22/EC, OJEU of 4.12.2020 No. L 409 p.1, hereinafter referred to as "RAD".

6 Hensler (2011: 306), Hensler et al. (2021: 1), Stadler et al. (2020: 1).

7 Durovic, Micklitz (2017: 81).

as well as (iii) group settlements existing in the Netherlands.[8] A broader approach to collective redress is presented by some prominent scholars who include not only court-based mechanisms but also non-judicial collective dispute resolution and public enforcement by government regulators or ombudsmen. Recently, Hodges and Voet also identified regulatory redress by the intervention of public enforcers.[9]

In the EU, a representative action was selected from the above described options. This mechanism has been chosen deliberately by policy makers to mark that the EU collective redress system is unique and distinct from the US approach. In this book, the representative actions, being an axis of the new EU collective redress framework, constitute a benchmark for the further analysis of the different mechanisms existing in the Member States and serving the purpose of consumer collective redress.

1.2 EU collective redress vs. US class action mechanism

Discussions on the shape of an EU collective redress system originated in the early nineties. At that time the class action system in the US was well developed and widely used in practice. Thus, many strategies and means that operated with success in the American legal system could have been transplanted to EU law. However, from the very beginning, the US-style class action system was widely (and unquestioningly) criticised by EU institutions.

To show how distinct the two approaches are, in EU law and policy, the term 'collective redress' was coined in opposition to the US-style class action system. Over the years, within the discussion of the desired shape of the EU model of collective redress, the European Commission debated that although the US class action system is the best-known example of collective redress, its functioning is highly controversial since it fosters a conflict of interests, and by extension, frivolous and abusive litigation.[10]

The Commission found that the most significant weakness of the US-style class action system is that it allows cases to be based on poor merit, on the one hand, and claimants need to receive adequate compensation since the money is diverted to their lawyers, on the other.[11] The American class action system was called a 'toxic cocktail' of several elements—punitive damages, contingency fees, opt-out and pre-trial discovery procedures. Therefore, class

8 Stoehr (2020: 1610–1614).

9 Hodges, Voet (2018: 1–2).

10 European Commission, Communication from the Commission to the European Parliament, the Council, the European Economic and Social Committee and the Committee of the Regions, "Towards a European Horizontal Framework for Collective Redress", 11.6.2013, COM (2013).

11 Hodges (2014: 71–75).

actions were rejected by the EU.[12] In order to avoid the problems mentioned above, the Commission advocated basing the EU model of collective redress on procedural mechanisms different from the US class action style, namely on representative and group actions.[13]

European objections voiced by the Commission against the US class action system have been reasonably criticised. Inherent in the voiced objection is the implication that the US system is unfairly tilted towards claimants. But the view is hard to support with objective evidence.[14] Several aspects of US law mentioned above generally apply to all civil litigation: punitive damages, contingency fees and expansive discovery.

Punitive damages provide plaintiffs with additional monetary relief beyond the value of the harm incurred to punish the wrongdoer and deter him and others from similar conduct in the future. That kind of damage is rarely awarded in the US, but the risk looms large for defendants in class actions. It is a myth, however, that punitive damage awards are all substantial. The decision on punitive damages lies with the jury or, in the cases without a jury, with the judge. The amount awarded by the jury is subjected to review by the judge, who, according to the observed trend, often reduces the award or removes it from the final judgment.[15] In the US, only a small percentage of the litigation reaches the verdict stage, and if the cases are settled, there are no punitive damages.[16] Further, as a result of a US Supreme Court ruling, punitive damages are capped at four times the compensatory damages.[17]

In the US, contingency fees promote a policy that facilitates access to the courts. It is strictly connected to the role of the lawyers in the class action.[18] In US class actions, there is no contract between attorneys and class members as opposed to European lawyers who are paid hourly or a flat rate. Instead, lawyers and law firms fund US class actions in exchange for a contingency fee.

12 European Commission in MEMO/08/741 to the Green Paper on Consumer Collective Redress – questions and answers, point nine stated "US-style class action is not envisaged. EU legal systems are very different from the US legal system, which results from a 'toxic cocktail' – a combination of several elements (punitive damages, contingency fees, opt-out, pre-trial discovery procedures)."

13 European Commission, Communication (2013) "Towards a European Horizontal Framework…" *op. cit.*

14 This observation is based on the notes I drafted on the occasion of prof. Deborah Hensler's Keynote Address during the seminar "Access to Justice and Class Action in England and Wales", organised at the University of Oxford on 6 May 2021. It was further confirmed by other American scholars at the Consumer Law Scholars Conference at Berkeley Center for Consumer Law and Economic Justice on 29 February 2024 and by class action practitioners during TACD Transatlantic Consumer Dialogue organised by National Association of Consumer Advocates on 20 May 2024 in Washington DC.

15 Vanleenhove (2017: 27).

16 *Op. cit.*, 29.

17 *State Farm Mutual Insurance Co. v. Campbell*, 538 U.S. 408 (2003).

18 Nagy (2019: 46–47).

These fees aim to promote access to justice and make class actions affordable. In the law and economics literature, there is explicit agreement that contingency fees can better tackle agency issues between the client and the lawyer than the hourly fee.[19] Lawyers who are paid hourly receive remuneration irrespective of whether they win the case. This may induce them to put too many hours into the case, delay it to obtain higher remuneration, and litigate cases with a low probability of success.[20] All of these risks are eliminated in the case of contingency fees. It must be noted that the court exercises control over contingency fees and any fee awarded is subject to court approval. Further, the class members receive notice of the requested fee award and may object to the amount of the fees as part of the class administration process. As a result of judicial oversight,[21] pure contingency fees fixed by lawyers, as they are classically understood, do not exist in the US.

Discovery in the US is intended to level the playing field between plaintiffs and defendants. The scope of discovery is not discretionary. Over the years, Supreme Court decisions and rule changes have narrowed the availability and scope of pre-trial discovery.[22] Over the past decade, the US Federal Rules of Civil Procedure governing discovery have attempted to rein in discovery. In 2015, Rule 26 was amended to emphasise proportionality limits in discovery and to list the factors that should be used to measure proportionality.[23]

Notwithstanding the European objections to the US class action system, it must be noted by some scholars in Europe that the practical importance of class action in the US is decreasing.[24] This trend could be confirmed in the latest case law of the US Supreme Court, which, among others, approved class action waivers in consumer and labour law contracts.[25]

1.3 Opt-in or opt-out?

One of the most controversial ingredients of the purported 'toxic cocktail' of the US class action system is the opt-out rule that permits named plaintiffs (and their chosen lawyers) to represent a group without the members first consenting to the action.[26] Under an opt-out system, the group comprises all the individuals who may have been harmed by the same or similar infringement unless they actively exclude themselves from the lawsuit. In such a case, they

19 Visscher, Faure (2021: 462–463) and the literature referred therein.
20 *Op. cit.*, p. 462.
21 Baker et al. (2015: electronic source); Eisenberg, Miller (2003: 2).
22 Miller (2018: 40).
23 Klonoff (2018: 1956).
24 Stadler (2021: 22).
25 *AT&T Mobility LLC v. Conception*, 563 U.S. 333 (2011).
26 In literature, the opt-out system is called "representation without authorization": see Nagy (2019: 45).

are not bound by the judgment and can pursue their claims individually.[27] As a result of the lack of specific authorisation for representation, the size of the group can be enormous; therefore, in case of class action success, the size of the compensation awarded to be paid by the defendant can be huge.

The main arguments voiced against the opt-out system in the EU include (i) constitutional concerns, (ii) lack of foundation in European legal traditions, (iii) technical difficulties in the identification of the affected group, and (iv) the risk of abusive litigation.[28] Firstly, it is argued that opt-out procedures derogate from the autonomy principle. The final judgment, binding on all class members who have yet to opt out, precludes future individual claims. However, without such a mechanism, numerous small claims would never go to court (because it is not beneficial), and the constitutional right of access to justice would be infringed. Secondly, the opt-out rule is already used in some EU Member States,[29] so the argument about this system being alien to EU legal traditions is unfounded. Thirdly, although the distribution of compensation might be complex in the opt-out system, there is a considerable branch of cases in which it is relatively easy (for example, identification of all individuals who entered the specific agreement with the same trader). Of course, identifying the group members is easier when pre-trial discovery is available, as discussed above in relation to US class action. Last but not least, no statistical data confirms causation between the opt-out rule and abusive or frivolous litigation. In contrast, such a phenomenon is not observed in any EU Member State where a collective redress system is already based on an opt-out mechanism.[30]

In the opt-in system, the group includes only those individuals who made an explicit disposition to be represented. Consequently, the judgment is binding only on those who opted in, while others remain free to pursue their claims individually. The opt-in procedures are perceived as more consistent with the Member States' legal and constitutional traditions, namely the principle of party autonomy.[31] However, when the claim's value is low—as seen in many consumer claims—it is unlikely that many individuals will invest their time to join the group action. Consequently, such an opt-in model provides less deterrence when traders impose small but illegal additional costs.[32] Further,

27 The legislation of most Member States, including Poland, imposes the opt-in system. The opt-out principle is applied by two Member States, namely the Netherlands and Portugal. In comparison, four Member States (Belgium, Bulgaria, Denmark and, in competition cases, also the UK) provide for a mixed system. See European Parliament, Collective redress…, *op. cit.*, pp. 22–27.

28 Nagy (2019: 23).

29 Hamulakowa (2018: 95–117).

30 For a brilliant, detailed comparative analysis of all the arguments, please see Nagy (2019: 23–44).

31 Amaro et al (2018:85).

32 Hensler (2016: 246).

identifying the group members is more manageable (they must expressly join group action). However, practice shows many problems with determining the group members in this model since group proceedings are cumbersome and long-lasting.

It is also possible to keep both opt-in and opt-out systems parallel or combine both models in one proceeding.[33] In the first situation, the judge typically decides which model is more suitable for the dispute. Opt-in proceedings might also be reserved for international disputes with opt-out for purely domestic ones. Further, a combined model might be used in a situation where individuals opt to be involved in a group action. However, in the proceedings, they opt out since, for example, they are not satisfied with the settlement proposal.

The choice between opt-in and opt-out options has been widely discussed in the literature. In line with my general observation, scholars reasonably favour the opt-out model since it is most effective. Such a trend is noticeable, especially from the law and economics perspective.[34] Visscher and Faure claim that the argument that the opt-out model is contrary to party autonomy is unconvincing because, due to rational apathy, this autonomy would not result in an individual claim anyway.[35] For the same reason, Ervo claims that the opt-out model, combined with compensatory relief, is considered the most efficient solution to deal with widespread and dispersed damages.[36] In favour of the opt-out model, Sahin proposes to include the requirement of adequate notice, aiming to reach each group member and provide them with information necessary to the collective action on their behalf and their right to opt out. She claims that with such an effective notice requirement, opt-out actions would be compatible with the right of access to the courts while preserving its ability to deliver compensation to many consumers.[37] Based on practical experiments, Nagy demonstrates no causation between the opt-out system and the 'litigation boom'; thus, the European fear of abusive litigation following the opt-out model is unjustified.[38]

EU institutions lacked consensus on the choice of one principle regarding the group's composition at the EU level. To this end, the European Commission recommended the opt-in model. It justified its standpoint, among others, by stating that it makes it possible to respect the right of a person to decide whether to participate and, thus, preserve the parties' autonomy.[39]

33 Hamulakowa (2018: 97).
34 Visscher, Faure (2021: 460).
35 *Op. cit.*
36 Ervo (2015: 167–200).
37 Sahin (2019: 148).
38 Nagy (2019: 37–38).
39 Commission Recommendation of 11 June 2013 on common principles for injunctive and compensatory redress mechanisms in the Member States concerning violation of rights granted

A different approach was articulated by the European Parliament, which favoured the opt-out or mixed system, leaving a margin of appreciation to national judges since it is more effective and even 'more justified in cases where the exercise of 'opt-in' would entail more damages, namely for the consumers, in terms of the cost of joining, and for the traders, in terms of the costs of notifying all parties involved.'[40] According to the findings of the study commissioned by the European Parliament, the decision on the choice of the variants in question should not be left to the discretion of the Member States. This approach, however, has not been adopted in RAD.[41]

1.4 Different routes to the EU consumer collective redress framework

The diversity of collective redress mechanisms in some Member States with respect to design, quality and operation, and the lack of them in another, gives rise to different levels of consumer law enforcement in the EU. Being aware of that fact, on the one hand, and noting the advantages and weaknesses of collective redress on the other, the European Commission[42] started to work on a framework for collective redress at the EU level.

In the 1990s, the EU legislature observed the need to ensure the protection of collective consumer interests in the EU. This issue was mentioned for the first time in 1996 in the Commission's Action Plan on consumer access to justice and the settlement of consumer disputes.[43] Simultaneously, along with the performance of the action plan, the Commission drafted Directive 98/27/EC on injunctions for the protection of consumer interests,[44] aimed at creating a mechanism that would make it possible to eliminate infringements of collective consumer interests. Directive 98/27/EC constituted a tool of procedural law used in a case of the infringement of rights of substantive law, granted in consumer directives attached to said act.[45]

under Union Law, 2013/396/EU, OJEU L 201/60, (hereinafter: Recommendation 2013/396/EU), para. 21–24.

40 Amaro et al (2018: 86).

41 *Ibidem*. In RAD a very cautious approach towards this question was adopted. As far as domestic actions are concerned, it is for the Member States to decide which model (opt-in or opt-out) to follow, whereas the opt-in model is imposed for cross-border representative actions. It is discussed in the section 1.6.2. in this chapter.

42 To be more specific, two Directorate-General: DG SANCO and DG COMP.

43 Communication from the Commission "Action Plan on consumer access to justice and settling consumer disputes in the internal market," 14.02.1996, COM (96)13 final.

44 Directive 98/27/EC of the European Parliament and of the Council of 19 May 1998 on injunctions for the protection of consumers' interests, OJEC, L 166/51.

45 Sieradzka (2008: electronic source).

Due to the amendments introduced to Directive 98/27/EC in 2009, it was repealed by Directive 2009/22/EC on injunctions for the protection of consumer interests.[46] Despite the legislature being presumably aware of the disadvantages of the existing mechanism, no significant amendments were introduced. The lack of fundamental changes was justified by the fact that the collective consumer redress model of that time was supposed to be complemented by another instrument, which would make it possible to claim damages for breach of competition law. In the white paper on damages actions for breach of EC antitrust rules (2008),[47] the Commission suggested introducing two collective redress mechanisms in competition law, allowing consumers and small businesses to obtain compensation for damages: representative actions brought by qualified entities such as consumer associations or state bodies and second opt-in collective actions. As a result, in 2009, the Commission prepared the legislative Proposal for the Directive on Collective Actions. However, the proposal was aborted due to strong resistance from the business environment and heavy pressure imposed on the Commission by some Member States.[48] One of the arguments voiced against the proposed mechanisms was the inconsistent approach to collective redress in the field of competition and consumer law, which was caused by the fact that two directorate-generals (DG), DG for Competition and DG for Health and Consumer Protection, had different concepts regarding the future shape of the collective redress system. While the first one favoured the introduction of a binding mechanism in the field of compensatory redress, the second was far more vague in its suggestions in this respect.[49] In order to provide coherent policy in this field, the commissioners for competition, consumer affairs and justice were requested to work together on further developments in the collective redress system.[50]

However, the proposal to introduce a legal instrument enabling the claim of competition law damages collectively remained controversial over the years.[51] To this end, to increase the chances of its adoption, the new Proposal for a Directive on Competition Damages of 2013 did not mention collective action at all.[52] The political solution adopted by the Commission was

46 Directive 2009/22/EC of the European Parliament and of the Council of 23 April 2009 on injunctions for the protection of consumers' interests, OJEU, L 110/30.

47 European Commission, White Paper on Damages Actions for Breach of EC antitrust rules, 02.04.2008, COM(2008) 165 final; see also: Sahin (2019: 41–42).

48 Hodges (2014:72), Sorabji (2014:74), Stadler (2013:483).

49 Compare European Commission, White Paper on Damages… (2008) *op. cit.* and European Commission, Green Paper on Consumer Collective Redress, 27.11.2008, COM(2008) 794 final.

50 Hodges (2014: 72), Stadler (2013: 483–484).

51 Sorabji (2014: 74).

52 Proposal for a Directive of the European Parliament and of the Council on specific rules governing actions for damages under national law for infringements of the competition law provisions

to separate the proposal for collective actions into a soft law instrument.[53] Thus, in 2013, the Commission issued its recommendation on common principles for injunctive and compensatory collective redress mechanisms.[54] The Commission indicated therein that all Member States should have collective redress mechanisms at the national level for both injunctive and compensatory relief.[55] The goal of this document was not to harmonise the national systems of collective redress but to introduce non-binding, general rules applicable to both court and out-of-court proceedings.[56] Recommendation 2013/396/EU identifies specific safeguards relating to either injunctive or compensatory collective redress,[57] as well as common principles for both types of redress. The last category includes, among other things, the principles regarding the legal standing to bring representative actions, the admissibility of collective actions, information on collective actions, the reimbursement of legal costs of the winning party, the funding of legal actions, and some general principles about cross-border cases.[58] According to the Commission, the safeguards in Recommendation 2013/396/EU aim to provide a barrier against abuse.[59] However, at the same time, this document allows Member States many exemptions, which hampers this goal. Although Recommendation 2013/396/EU was supposed to do its work, the latest comparative studies show that most of the Member States did not follow the principles set out by the Commission. Despite the existing guidelines, collective redress mechanisms are still significantly varied.[60] Therefore, according to the predominant view, the recommendation itself did not contribute to establishing a standard, pan-European model of collective consumer redress.[61]

When the Dieselgate scandal occurred in 2015, it became clear that the EU needed a more coherent mechanism that enabled effective collective redress. In 2018, the European Commission issued 'A New Deal for Consumers'[62]that proposed a new legislative package as an answer to the new challenges of

---

of the Member States and of the European Union, COM(2013) 404. See also: E. Sahin (2019: 47).

53 Ioannidou, (2011:61).

54 Recommendation 2013/396/EU, *op. cit.*

55 *Ibidem*, Art. 2.

56 Voet (2014: 97–128), Hodges (2014: 78).

57 See Piszcz (2017: 223–250) for compensatory collective redress.

58 Recommendation 2013/396/EU, points 4–18.

59 *Ibidem*, para. 10.

60 European Parliament, Study on Collective redress in the Member States of the European Union, 2018.

61 Sorabji (2014: 75), Hodges,Voet (2018: 43).

62 Communication from the Commission to the European Parliament, the Council and the European Economic and Social Committee, "A New Deal for Consumers," 11.04.2018, COM (2018) 183 final, (hereinafter: "A New Deal for Consumers").

consumer policy.[63] A New Deal for Consumers aimed at, among other things, providing better redress opportunities for consumers, supporting effective enforcement and enhancing the cooperation of public authorities in a fair and safe single market.[64] In this respect, the Commission presented a Proposal for RAD.[65] In that Proposal, the Commission wanted to modernise the existing model for the protection of the collective interests of consumers in the European Union, which, in principle, should improve the efficiency of collective consumer redress. The main innovation provided by the Commission was the combination of collective injunctive measures and redress measures. After years of discussions on the Proposal, RAD was adopted in 2020. It was transposed by Member States by 25 December 2022 and applicable from 25 June 2023. However, there were some Member States (regrettably including Poland) that did not implement RAD in a timely manner.[66]

1.4 Challenges to consumer law enforcement under Directive 2009/22/EC[67]

The current shape of EU consumer collective redress established by RAD builds on legal solutions provided in Directive 2009/22/EC. The latter, however, 'did not sufficiently address the challenges of relating to the enforcement of consumer law.'[68] In order to determine whether RAD responded to those challenges, it is vital to indicate the weaknesses of the consumer law enforcement model provided by Directive 2009/22/EC. To comprehensively assess whether the new solutions 'strengthen procedural mechanisms for the protection of collective interests of consumers,' as is indicated in RAD, it is indispensable first to discuss the critical problems observed under Directive 2009/22/EC. It is the only way to find out if (yes) how far the gaps identified have been rectified by RAD.

1.4.1 The limited spectrum of legal remedies

First and foremost, under Directive 2009/22/EC, the only tool serving the purpose of exercising consumer rights was the 'action for an injunction for the protection of consumer interests' and no compensatory redress measures were provided.[69] The only legal consequence of the injunction procedure

63 Jabłonowska, Namysłowska (2018: 11), Kowalczyk-Zagaj (2018: 120).
64 "A New Deal for Consumers," *op. cit.*, p. 4.
65 Proposal for a Directive on Representative Actions, *op. cit.*
66 See: Chapter 3.
67 This section builds in the research findings drawing on the author's publication: Mucha (2019b).
68 RAD, rec. 5.
69 Directive 2009/22/EC, *op. cit.*, Art. 1.

available under Directive 2009/22/EC was the prohibition of the trader from continuing the infringement. The directive did not provide any further remedies to remove the consequences of the infringement of consumer rights. The European Commission emphasised that 'as a general rule, the injunction procedure introduced by the Directive does not enable consumers who have suffered harm because of an illicit practice to obtain compensation.'[70]

This limited effect of the injunction procedure designed by Directive 2009/22/EC on consumer redress possibilities constituted a significant problem that hampered the mechanism's effectiveness. The fact that consumers could not seek compensation together with seeking an injunction and, therefore, were forced to commence separate individual proceedings posed unnecessary litigation risks and increased costs not only for consumers but also for the whole justice system. It also discouraged consumers from pursuing their claims collectively since even a successful action for an injunction might not have resulted in positive financial implications.

It was reported that in most Member States, consumers cannot rely on injunction orders. To claim compensation, they must bring a separate claim for damages (individually or collectively).[71] In many Member States, the courts adjudicating compensation claims are not bound by a previous injunction order.[72] Consumers have to prove the infringement (anew), the damage and the link between the infringement and the damage. Only in some Member States can consumers rely on injunction orders in their follow-on action for compensation, where they then have to prove only the amount of the damage suffered.[73]

1.4.2 Costs of the proceedings

One of the shortcomings of Directive 2009/22/EC was that it did not regulate the issue of costs linked to the injunction proceedings but it left it to the discretion of Member States. In order to prevent abusive litigation and frivolous

70 Report from the Commission to the European Parliament and the Council concerning the application of Directive 2009/22/EC of the European Parliament and of the Council on injunctions for the protection of consumers' interest, 6.11.2012, COM (2012) 635 final (hereinafter: "Report on the application of Directive 2009/22/EC (2012)"), p. 9.

71 Report from the Commission to the European Parliament, the Council and the European Economic and Social Committee on the implementation of the Commission Recommendation of 11 June 2013 on common principles for injunctive and compensatory collective redress mechanisms in the Member States concerning violation of rights granted under Union Law (2013/396/EU), 25.1.2018, COM (2018) 40 final (hereinafter: "Report on the implementation of the Commission Recommendation 2013/396/EU (2018)"), p. 18.

72 *Ibidem.*

73 The Commission Report (2018) revealed that "In Denmark, Belgium, and Italy it is possible to rely on an injunctions decision in a follow-on collective action in consumer law cases [...] In Netherlands follow-on actions are possible not as a matter of law but rather of practice."

claims, the European Commission recommended following the principle of reimbursement of legal costs to the winning party (the so-called 'loser pays principle').[74] The latest report showed that Member States broadly apply this principle in their civil procedural law.[75] As a result, in the light of the necessity to reimburse the costs of the opposing party, the claims are brought mainly in these cases in which the probability of winning by the qualified entity is high. In many Member States, the qualified entities have a Hobson's choice: if they win the case they may still be obliged to pay the costs of proceedings if the losing defendant cannot pay the costs.[76] The research shows that the financial risk linked to the proceedings for an injunction is the most crucial obstacle that limits the number of actions for an injunction brought by qualified entities. Therefore, it considerably impairs the effectiveness of the collective redress mechanism in the whole EU.[77]

1.4.3 Limited effect of the ruling

Another significant problem related to the use of actions for an injunction was the limited effect of the ruling.[78] Studies conducted by the European Commission confirmed that in most Member States, an injunction order is issued concerning the case and the parties involved. This means it binds only the qualified entity that brought an action for an injunction and the defendant trader (*inter partes* effect).[79] In practice, if one trader infringes on the rights of consumers and the infringement is identical to the infringement committed by another trader, confirmed by an earlier judgment, the consumer cannot rely on the previous injunction order but must prove the infringement anew. This poses problems for the effectiveness of an injunction order, and therefore, it increases the litigation risk and causes costs to the justice system.[80]

Only some of the Member States, in their legal orders, extended the effects of the decisions issued as a result of an action for an injunction to other parties (*erga omnes* effect), in particular concerning the nullity of unfair contract

74 Recommendation 2013/396/EU, *op. cit.*, para. 13.

75 All Member States with collective redress mechanisms, except Luxembourg, follow the "loser pays" principle in their civil procedural laws. See: European Commission, Report on the implementation of the Commission Recommendation 2013/396/EU (2018), *op. cit.* p. 8.

76 Report on the application of Directive 2009/22/EC (2012), p. 11.

77 European Commission, Staff Working Document: Report of the Fitness Check on consumer and marketing law directives (REFIT), 23.05.2017, SWD 2017 (208) final and SWD 2017 (209) final (hereinafter: "Fitness Check (2017)"), p. 103.

78 Report on the application of Directive 2009/22/EC (2012), *op. cit.*, pp. 13–16.

79 Report on the application of Directive 98/27/EC (2008), *op. cit.*, p. 9; Report on the application of Directive 2009/22/EC (2012), *op. cit.*, p. 14.

80 Fitness Check (2017), *op. cit.*, p. 104.

terms.[81] Extending the effects of injunctions beyond the individual case has the advantage of preventing repeated use of that term.[82] However, some national courts had doubts regarding the compliance of such regulation of national law with EU law, especially regarding Directive 93/13/EEC on unfair terms in consumer contracts.[83] Therefore, this issue was examined by the Court of Justice of the European Union (CJEU).

For the very first time, this question was analyzed by the CJEU in case C-472/10 *Invitel*,[84] where the proceedings before the CJEU commenced due to a reference for a preliminary ruling lodged by a Hungarian court. The reference was made in the context of public interest proceedings brought by the Hungarian national consumer protection authority (NFH) against Invitel—a telephone network operator. NFH alleged that Invitel used unfair terms in contracts concluded with consumers, which made consumers pay fees that had not initially been agreed upon between the parties. The Hungarian national consumer protection authority declared the contested term null and void on the grounds of being unfair and automatic. It imposed a retroactive reimbursement to the subscribers of the amounts wrongly invoiced. The national court was unsure whether it could declare the invalidity of an unfair term concerning all the consumers who have concluded a contract with unfair contract terms or only those consumers who are a party to the proceedings.

When answering this preliminary question, the CJEU recognised that consumers are in a weak position towards the trader with respect to both his bargaining power and his level of knowledge.[85] Consequently, consumers agree to the terms drawn up in advance by the trader without being able to influence the content of those terms. The CJEU referred to Article 6 of Directive 93/13/EEC, which provides that unfair terms shall, as provided for under the national law, not be binding for the consumer and stated that this provision aims to replace the formal balance of the contracting parties and to re-establish equality between them.[86] At the same time, the extension of the effects of an injunction to all consumers is justified due to the deterrent nature and dissuasive purpose of the action for an injunction.[87] Therefore, the CJEU adjudicated that the declaration of an unfair contract term's invalidity affects all consumers who concluded with the seller or supplier concerning a contract

81 Report on the application of Directive 98/27/EC (2008), *op. cit.*, p. 9; Report on the application of Directive 2009/22/EC (2012), *op. cit.*, p.14.

82 The Opinion of the Advocate General, case C-427/10 Invitel, ECLI:EU:C:2011:806, para. 69.

83 Council Directive 93/13/EEC of 5 April 1993 on unfair terms in consumer contracts, OJEC L95/29.

84 Judgment of the Court of Justice of the European Union dated 26 April 2012, C-472/10 *Nemzeti Fogyasztóvédelmi Hatóság v. Invitel Távközlési Zrt*, ECLI: EU:C:2012:242.

85 *Ibidem*, para. 33.

86 *Ibidem*, para. 34.

87 *Ibidem*, para. 37.

to which the same terms apply, including those not party to the injunction proceedings.[88]

Moreover, the CJEU stated that Directive 93/13/EEC does not preclude

> where the unfair nature of a term in the general business conditions has been acknowledged in such proceedings, national courts are required, of their motion, and also about the future, to take such action thereon as is provided for by national law in order to ensure that the consumers who have concluded a contract [...] will not be bound by that term.[89]

By the above, the CJEU approved the extension of *res judicata* of the decision on declaring the unfairness of a contract term to consumers who are not party to the proceedings. However, this obligation is imposed only on national courts of those Member States that recognise the *erga omnes* effect of an injunction.[90]

The question of the extension of the legal effects of an injunction order as regards other parties was also discussed by the CJEU in case C-119/15 *Partner*.[91] The judgment was issued due to a reference for a preliminary ruling requested by a Polish court. The referring court asked whether a judicial decision, having the force of law, which declared the contract terms unlawful and, as a result, had them entered into the register of unlawful standard contract terms, can have the effect not only on the trader being a party to the proceedings, but also in relation to other traders who use identical unlawful standard contract terms. In the case in question, the Polish court adjudicated on the appeal of Biuro Partner against the decision of the President of the Office of Competition and Consumer Protection (UOKiK) issued in an administrative procedure (the court of first instance upheld the original UOKiK decision). In the administrative decision, the President of UOKiK found that Biuro Partner, in its standard business conditions, used terms that were considered equivalent to terms previously declared unlawful and consequently entered into the public register of unfair terms. The President of UOKiK stated that those terms harmed the collective interests of consumers and imposed a fine on the company. The Polish court doubted such a decision since Biuro Partner did not participate in the proceedings in which the standard terms were declared unlawful and consequently entered into the public register.[92]

88 *Ibidem*, para. 44.
89 *Ibidem*.
90 Keirsblick (2013: 1473).
91 Judgment of the Court of Justice of the European Union dated 21 December 2016, C-119/15 *Biuro podróży 'Partner' sp. z o.o. sp. k. v., Prezes UOKiK*, ECLI:EU:C:2016:987.
92 For details see: Luzak (2017:123), Namysłowska (2017:194), Wyżykowski (2018:112)

The CJEU, however, adjudicated that the extended effect of the entry into the public register of unfair terms does not contradict EU law on the condition that the trader is vested with the relevant procedural guarantees.[93] The main requirement here is to ensure that the trader has an effective judicial remedy both against the decision declaring that the terms are equivalent to the terms entered into said register (in terms of the question of whether those terms are substantively identical and having regard in particular to their harmful effects for consumers) and against the decision stating the amount of the fine imposed.[94]

Applying the reasoning presented by the CJEU in the cases *Invitel* and *Partner*, it may be argued that the extension of the effects of an injunction order both on all consumers affected by the unfair contract terms and on the traders who use such terms in consumer contracts is to be welcomed at the EU level. However, the decision regarding the legal effects of the injunction is left at the discretion of the Member States. In both cases, the CJEU does not impose the obligation on the Member States to recognise the *erga omnes* effect of an injunction order, but it states that such wording of the national law does not contradict EU law.[95]

1.4.4 Limited application of cross-border actions

One of the most critical problems exposed by Directive 2009/22/EC is the minimal application of existing tools to counter cross-border infringements. Directive 2009/22/EC, following Directive 98/27/EC, permitted the qualified entities of Member State A to bring an action in Member State B if the latter, by trading with consumers in Member State A, were in breach of consumer law. Thus, the qualified entities are vested with legal standing before foreign courts. The court in Member State B would hear and decide the case without questioning the legal standing of the qualified entity of Member State A.

However, it was demonstrated by the Commission in the reports that the proposed concept of cross-border litigation is not used in practice. By 2008, only one qualified entity from the UK (the Office of Fair Trading) used this mechanism in two cases, bringing an action for an injunction to the courts of Belgium and the Netherlands.[96] The main reasons for the minimal use of such cross-border litigation are the costs of bringing an action, the complexity and length of the procedure, as well as the limited scope of the injunction procedure (injunction is mandatory only concerning the case and the parties in

93 *Ibidem*, para. 47.

94 *Ibidem*.

95 Wyżykowski (2018: 114–115).

96 Report on the application of Directive 98/27/EC (2008), *op. cit.* p. 6.

question and is limited in terms of the national scope).[97] Even though between 2008 and 2012, the number of cross-border cases increased (only around 70 injunctions with cross-border dimensions and 5,632 actions in total), most of them were based on something other than the concept provided in Directive 2009/22/WE.[98] Although established abroad, the traders were sued in the country where they directed their commercial activity, the consumer's country of origin. The qualified entities brought actions for an injunction in their language, own jurisdiction and in line with the applicable national law. This allowed them to avoid many practical problems, such as language barriers or difficulty identifying and assessing the trader data abroad.

The latest data confirmed that injunctions requiring the cessation or prohibition of an infringement are still not used in cross-border cases, and the qualified entities from different Member States do not cooperate enough with one another in order to exchange good practices or develop common strategies to counter widespread infringements.[99]

1.5 Addressing the problems in the Proposal for RAD

Outcomes revealed in the report on the implementation of the Commission Recommendation 2013/396/EU published in 2018 confirmed the concerns articulated by some scholars as regards the abidance of the safeguards provided in Recommendation 2013/396/EU.[100] It leaves no doubt that the non-binding instrument cannot provide procedural coherence and ensure a homogenous landscape of collective redress in the EU. Although the European Commission recommended that all Member States have collective redress mechanisms at the national level for injunctive and compensatory relief, nine Member States did not introduce mechanisms for compensatory collective claims.[101]

However, it was also clear that the procedural mechanism provided in Directive 2009/22/EC—action for an injunction—is not a sufficient instrument to enforce consumer rights. Keeping in mind the mentioned lack of legislation in this field at the national level, on the one hand, and being aware of the problems hampering the effectiveness of the injunction procedure as designed by Directive 2009/22/EC, on the other, the European Commission

97 *Ibidem*, pp. 6–9.

98 Report on the application of Directive 2009/22/EC (2012), *op. cit.*, p. 7.

99 Fitness Check (2017), *op. cit.* p. 102; Explanatory Memorandum of European Commission, Proposal for a directive of the European Parliament and of the Council on representative actions for the protection of the collective interests of consumers, and repealing Directive 2009/22/EC, 11.4.2018, COM(2018), 184 final, p. 8.

100 Stadler (2013: 488), Sorabji (2014: 75), Hodges (2014: 78), Howells (2017: electronic resource), Money-Kyrle (2016: 251).

101 Report on the implementation of the Commission Recommendation 2013/396/EU (2018), *op. cit.*, p. 3.

commenced works on new legislation that allows modernisation to complement the existing system of the protection of collective interests of consumers in the EU.

Having this in mind, in the Proposal for RAD the Commission tried to combine the procedural mechanisms existing in Directive 2009/22/EC (that is, the action for an injunction) and mechanisms that, due to a political consensus, were finally included in Recommendation 2013/396/EU, namely the action for compensation. In this sense, the Proposal for RAD constitutes a concept continuum that has never been included in a binding act due to political resistance. In what follows the Proposal for RAD is examined as to whether it answered the problems that have hindered the effectiveness of existing mechanisms for collective redress.

1.5.1 Injunctive and redress measures

The most significant change included in the Proposal for RAD was the extension of the measures the qualified entities may seek within one or many proceedings. Following the Directive 2009/22/EC pattern, the Proposal for RAD provided that the qualified entities may seek an injunction order (interim or definite measure) to stop or prohibit the trader's practice.[102] The significant change, however, was caused by introducing a different measure to eliminate the continuing effect of infringement. In this respect, it provided for the possibility to seek compensatory redress, or—in line with the terminology used in the Proposal—representative actions for compensation. In the redress order, a trader may be obliged to provide for, among other things, compensation, repair, replacement, price reduction, contract termination, or reimbursement of the price paid (compensatory redress mechanisms).[103]

The Proposal for RAD introduced the principle according to which proceedings initiated by collective actions for compensation, which were adjudicated in favour of consumers, shall be finalised with a redress order. Only under particular circumstances—instead of a redress order—can the court or administrative body issue a declaratory decision regarding the trader's liability towards the consumers harmed by an infringement of EU law. This discretion was granted only in duly justified cases where, due to the characteristics of the individual harm to consumers concerned, the quantification of individual redress is complex and thus ineffective to be quantified within representative action.[104] Such a declaratory decision may be directly relied upon in subsequent redress actions (both individual and collective).[105]

102 Proposal for RAD, *op. cit.*, Art. 5.
103 Proposal for RAD, *op. cit.*, Art. 6.
104 Proposal for RAD, *op. cit.*, Art. 5.
105 Explanatory Memorandum to the Proposal for RAD, *op. cit.*, point 1.

The possibility of issuing a declaratory decision was strictly excluded in two cases regarding mass harm.[106] The first related to cases where the consumers concerned by the infringement are identifiable and suffered harm comparable to the one caused by the same practice concerning the time or purchase.[107] The second one concerned cases where consumers suffered an insignificant loss, and it would be disproportionate to distribute the redress to them.[108] In such cases, the redress shall be diverted to public purposes serving the collective interests of consumers, such as awareness campaigns, consumer legal aid funds, or consumer movements.[109]

1.5.2 Legal costs and funding qualified entities

A major obstacle hampering the effectiveness of the injunction procedure provided in Directive 2009/22/EC is the high costs of proceedings commenced by the action for an injunction. Under the Proposal for RAD, this problem was solved only to some extent. On the one hand, the Proposal stated that the Member States should ensure that procedural costs related to representative actions shall not constitute financial obstacles to the qualified entities and this shall be achieved by limiting the costs of judicial and administrative proceedings, granting access to legal aid and providing the entities with public funding.[110] On the other hand, however, the Proposal for RAD left it to the discretion of Member States to regulate the cost of the injunction proceedings. According to the Proposal, this act should not affect the national rules concerning allocating procedural costs.[111]

It is worth noting that the legal framework proposed still applied the principle according to which the costs of the injunction procedure were to be borne by the qualified entity bringing representative action. At the same time, the Proposal for RAD stated that the procedural costs of the proceedings shall not prevent the qualified entities from effectively exercising the right to seek redress. Although it did not regulate this question directly, it gave some guidance as regards the possibility of funding of the qualified entities.

An interesting innovation introduced in the Proposal for RAD was the possibility of financing the activity of the qualified entities from the private sector, among other things, from the business environment. Member States might have decided whether only some of the qualified entities financed by third parties will be allowed to seek all the redress measures available (including

106 *Ibidem.*
107 Proposal for RAD, *op. cit.*, Art. 5.
108 *Ibidem.*
109 Proposal for RAD, *op. cit.*, rec. 21.
110 *Ibidem*, Art. 15.
111 *Ibidem*, rec. 4.

compensatory collective redress). Regarding the entities seeking compensatory collective redress, the EU legislator provided an additional obligation to declare the source of the funds used for its activity in general and the funds it uses to support the action.[112] Additionally, the qualified entities had to demonstrate that they have sufficient financial resources to meet adverse costs should the action fail. At the same time, the Proposal for RAD prohibited third-party funding in case of actions brought against a defendant who is a competitor of the fund provider or against a defendant on whom the fund provider is dependent.

1.5.3 Duration of the proceedings

Following the need to ensure the effectiveness of the proceedings, the European Commission provided that representative actions shall be treated with due expediency.[113] By exception, a representative action for an injunction order in interim measure shall have been treated according to an accelerated procedure. This procedure aims to ensure that any further harm caused by a trader's practice, subject to representative action, may be prevented as quickly as possible.[114] However, the Commission needed to provide guidance on the course of those proceedings and provide any difference between both types. There being no precise regulations in this respect, it is doubtful whether it will constitute a turning point, making it possible to shorten the time of the proceedings.

A promising solution proposed by the Commission was the 'one-stop-shop' procedure allowing qualified entities to seek both injunctive and collective measures within a single proceeding[115] This provision aimed to increase the procedural effectiveness of representative actions. This solution could have significantly shortened the proceedings' duration if adequately implemented. The problem of rational apathy of consumers could be significantly reduced if they could obtain redress without the necessity to bring a follow-up action. However, it shall be noted that this proposal brought many doubts to those Member States, including Poland,[116] in which there exists a dual system of injunctive and collective measures.

112 *Ibidem*, Art. 7.
113 *Ibidem*, Art. 12.
114 Explanatory Memorandum to the Proposal for RAD, *op. cit.*, point. 5.
115 Proposal for RAD, *op. cit.*, Art. 5 (4).
116 Mucha (2019: 17).

1.5.4 The final effect of the decision

In cases where a one-stop-shop procedure is not possible and injunctive and compensatory measures are sought separately, the European Commission proposed an interesting solution to raise the efficiency of representative actions. In line with Article 10 of the Proposal, the final decision of the court or administrative authority, including the final injunction order, shall have constituted a refutable presumption of that infringement for follow-up actions seeking redress. Similarly, when the final declaratory decision regarding the trader's liability towards the harmed consumers is issued, and the follow-up actions for redress are to be brought individually, such a decision irrefutably establishes the same trader's liability for the same infringement. This is particularly important since, as demonstrated above, group litigations are lengthy and the duration of the proceedings is one reason consumers want to avoid going to court.

1.5.5 Cross-border representative actions

The Proposal for RAD keeps the model of cross-border representative actions, which permits qualified entities from Member State A to apply to the courts or administrative authorities in Member State B if the traders from B breach consumer law while trading with consumers from Member State A.[117] In the same way, as under Directive 2009/22/EC, Member States would have to present to the Commission a list of qualified entities designated in advance.

Notably, specific procedures for cross-border representative actions have yet to be proposed. Lack of regulation in this respect implies for the qualified entities the necessity to get acquainted with the relevant legal regulations of another Member State (judicial or administrative, depending on the legal order of the Member States). In the same way as it is practised under the current law, it will entail some financial consequences, namely, the qualified entity must bear the costs of the preparation of the claim, court fees, remuneration of the lawyers from different jurisdictions, or translation costs. Additionally, bringing cross-border claims will likely be hindered by uncertainty regarding the choice of applicable law governing the dispute in point. The Proposal for RAD does not provide or refer to any private international law rules regarding the competent courts, the recognition and enforcement of the judgments, or the choice of applicable law, and it does not refer to any other act of EU law.[118] Leaving this area unregulated, the Proposal follows the old pattern set in Recommendation 2013/396/EU.[119]

117 Proposal for RAD, *op. cit.*, Art. 16.
118 Biard (2018: 201).
119 Stadler (2013: 484).

The legal situation of consumers can be even more complex in the case of representative actions brought by the same qualified entity to protect the collective interests of consumers from different Member States. The Proposal for RAD allows for bringing an action by a single qualified entity on behalf of consumers from different Member States affected (or likely to be affected) by the same infringement committed by a trader. Such cross-border action may also be brought to the competent court or administrative authority by several representative authorities acting jointly. Although introducing the possibility to commence such proceedings is justified by the need to ensure the procedure's effectiveness, the lack of guidance on the course of such cross-border proceedings is astonishing since it will pose many legal difficulties.

1.5.6 Business concerns

Finding a solution that allows for consumer access to justice and at the same time prohibits abusive litigation was a big challenge. It was clear from the beginning of legislative process that the stakeholders interests were very different. The proposed legislative framework has been strongly supported by consumer organisations such as BEUC and widely criticised by the business industry. Despite the assurances declared by the European Commission,[120] the main concern articulated by the business sector was that using representative actions would give rise to abuse of collective litigation. It is undisputed that to balance the interests of consumers seeking redress and the rights of traders, the legal framework for collective actions shall include some procedural safeguards to prevent this legal instrument's misuse. The Commission complied with traders in that the Proposal for RAD should not incentivise competitors, third-party investors and law firms to litigate against companies at the expense of consumers. However, some stakeholders believed the Proposal failed to provide many safeguards to minimise the risk of abusive litigation. They argued that many of such elements included in the 2013 Commission's recommendation on collective redress[121] were not transferred to the Proposal for RAD.[122] Some of the most problematic issues in this respect will be discussed below, since they impacted the final shape of RAD.

120 Explanatory Memorandum to the Proposal for RAD, *op. cit.*

121 Stadler (2013: 483); Sorabji (2014: 62).

122 European Commission, Recommendation of 11.06.2013 on common principles for injunctive and compensatory redress mechanisms in the Member States concerning violations of rights granted under Union Law, 2013/396/EU, OJEU of 26.7.2013, L 201 p. 60.

1.5.6.1 Risk of abusive litigation

Predictably, the first concern voiced by the business environment related to the possibility of consumers seeking compensatory measures. The industry was firmly against introducing such measures from the beginning of the Commission's work on the collective redress framework. However, when it became clear that after decades of heated debate, the redress measures would finally be provided, the business environment argued that the scope of compensatory measures should be significantly limited. Admittedly, among others, the Proposal for RAD did not provide that the compensation shall cover the actual harm suffered by the consumers and it did not explicitly exclude punitive damages from its scope. Although the Commission noticed that punitive damages could lead to overcompensation in favour of the consumers, it did not explicitly prohibit such damages in the main body of the Proposal for RAD.[123] Instead it referred to the punitive damages only in its recitals, stating that such damages should be avoided (and not prohibited).

Furthermore, the Proposal for RAD never explicitly referred to the 'loser-pays principle,' according to which the party that loses a collective redress action reimburses the necessary legal costs the winning party bears. Instead of such a principle, it included the Member State's obligation to ensure that the costs of the representative action may be recovered from the trader where the action is successful (Article 15 point 2). Moreover, the Proposal neither referred to the lawyers' remuneration nor specified any calculation method. It ignored the issue of contingency fees, which are calculated as a percentage of amounts awarded, and—according to the business lobby—such information would undoubtedly constitute an incentive to initiate litigation.

According to some stakeholders, 'leaving the choice of safeguards to Member States will lead to significant inconsistency, provoking a 'race to the bottom' in safeguards and consequently leading to forum shopping.'[124] Furthermore, the lack of necessary safeguards left defendants, including small and medium-sized enterprises, 'even more exposed to the risks of misuse than under the US Class Action system.'[125] Comparison of the Commission's Proposal for RAD with the US class action system was particularly

123 Rec. 4 and 17 of the Proposal for RAD.

124 Joint Statement of the associations AIRE, Airlines 4 Europe, AmCham EU, Bitkom, CER, Digitaleurope, EDiMA, EEPIA, European Banking Federation, European Justice Forum, IATA, MedTech Europe, US Chamber Institute for Legal Reform, *Directive on Representative Actions The European Commission's proposal risks undermining civil justice systems to the detriment of consumers across Europe* http://www.cer.be/sites/default/files/publication/181008_Joint%20Statement_Proposal%20for%20a%20Directive%20on%20Representative%20actions.pdf (access: 5.04.2023).

125 *Ibidem*.

controversial bearing in mind that for many years, the Commission kept recalling that the US class action system is not envisaged in Europe.[126]

1.5.6.2 Missing criteria for qualified entities

Another argument voiced against the Proposal for RAD was a lack of precise requirements for recognition as qualified entities. In line with Article 4(1) of the Proposal for RAD, qualified entities shall have satisfied only very general criteria, according to which they: (i) shall be adequately constituted according to the law of the Member State, (ii) shall have a legitimate interest in ensuring that the provisions of the EU law covered by the proposal are complied with, and (iii) they shall have a non-profit character. Regarding the second condition, the business lobby emphasised that such legitimate interest cannot be only claimed on the surface. However, the entity shall demonstrate it and be capable of being verified by the court.[127] As it is additionally claimed, qualified entities shall have proved their stability and seriousness by the minimum period of existence to avoid abuses.

A solution that was clearly against the interests of the business environment was the possibility of constituting qualified entities *ad hoc*, with the sole purpose of bringing a representative action, which was permitted under Article 4(2) of the Proposal for RAD. Moreover, the Proposal did not explain how the court or an administrative body shall demonstrate and verify the non-profit character of qualified entities. It did not prohibit lawyers and litigation funders from being members of qualified entities, which, according to traders, entailed a risk that lawyers would use qualified entities for their profit-making activities.[128]

126 European Commission, Green Paper on consumer collective redress, COM (2008) 794 final.

127 *See*: European Savings Bank Group, *Position on the proposal for a Directive on representative actions for the protection of the collective interests of consumers and repealing Directive 2009/22/EC*, https://www.wsbiesbg.org/SiteCollectionDocuments/ESBG_position_proposal_on_collective_interests_of_consumers_final.pdf (access: 5.04.2023).

128 Conversely, legal professionals claim that limiting the collective redress process to designated organisations reduces access to justice and is detrimental to consumers. *See*: Council of Bars and Law Societies of Europe, *Position on the Proposal for a Directive on representative actions for the protection of the collective interests of consumers, and repealing Directive 2009/22/EC 24/09/2018*, https://www.ccbe.eu/fileadmin/speciality_distribution/public/documents/ACCESS_TO_JUSTICE/ATJ_Position_papers/EN_ATJ_20180924_CCBE-position-on-the-Proposal-for-a-Directive-on-representative-actions-for-the-protection-of-the-collective-interests-of-consumers-and-repealing-Directive-200922EC.pdf (access: 5.04.2023).

Likewise, there were many doubts concerning the possibility of third-party funding. In line with the Proposal for RAD, Member States might have decided whether the qualified entities financed by third parties will be allowed to seek all the redress measures available (including compensatory collective redress) or whether this right is only granted to some of them. As regards the entities seeking compensatory collective redress, the Commission provided an additional obligation to declare the source of the funds used for their activity in general and the funds they use to support the action.[129] The Proposal for RAD prohibited third-party funding in case of actions brought against a defendant who is a competitor of the fund provider or against a defendant on whom the fund provider is dependent. However, although the Commission suggested that imposing such transparency over the funding source will prevent abusive litigation, it did not specify how courts or administrative bodies can verify it. This, in turn, entailed a risk of using qualified entities by one company to act against its competitors.

1.5.6.3 Uncertainty in terms of consumer mandate to initiate representative action

The Proposal for RAD made it unclear how consumers should join the group to be represented. On the one hand, it stated that to obtain injunctive orders, qualified entities shall not have to obtain the mandate of the individual consumers concerned.[130] Such wording might have suggested that the opt-out rule is the governing principle regarding injunctive redress. On the other hand, the Proposal did not refer to the necessity of having a consumer mandate to seek compensatory redress. This left the decision on the choice of the opt-in or opt-out model for compensatory redress at the discretion of Member States.

One unsurprising scenario was that the business environment was firmly against introducing the opt-out principle.[131] As mentioned above, the number of consumers represented within the representative action could be significant, in line with this procedure. They are not obliged to grant consent to be represented. Instead, they are included automatically since they have been harmed by the same or similar infringement. Unless they withdraw the claim,

129 Proposal for RAD, *op. cit.*, Art. 7

130 Proposal for RAD, *op. cit.*, Art. 5 (2)

131 Business Europe, US Chamber Institute for Legal Reform, Eurochambers, EuroCommerce, SME United, EDiMA, Insurance Europe, European Banking Federation, EFPIA, ESBG, FEDMA, Word Federation of Advertisers, AmChamEU, European Justice Forum, Airlines for Europe, *Joint Business Statement on the Proposal on Representative Actions (Collective Redress)*,

https://www.ebf.eu/wp-content/uploads/2018/12/Joint-Business-Statement-on-Representative-Actions-proposal-collective-redress-November-2018.pdf (access: 5.04.2023).

consumers are bound by the judgment and entitled to compensation if such is awarded. As a result, in the opt-out system, it could have been reasonably expected that the total compensation awarded to consumers be higher, contrary to the trader's interests.

1.5.7 Searching for a consensus in the trilogue

Many concerns of the business industry discussed above were shared by other EU institutions dealing with the Commission's Proposal for RAD at the later stages of the legislative process. In March 2019, the European Parliament adopted a legislative resolution acknowledging some stakeholder requests, including the business environment.[132] The resolution suggested an explicit prohibition of punitive damages (Article 6 para. 4b) and contingency fees (Article 15a). It also required Member States to introduce the loser-pays principle (Article 7a). With regard to third-party funding, in its resolution, the European Parliament obliged the qualified entities to disclose to the court all details of their financing to demonstrate that they are not in a conflict of interest. Qualified entities would disclose how they are financed, organised and managed to the public. Courts would be allowed to declare a representative action inadmissible where a third party funds it and where that funding would influence the decision of a qualified entity, including its decision to initiate a representative action, and where the defendant is a competitor of the fund provider (Article 7 para. 2). In line with the amendments proposed by the European Parliament, Member States would not be allowed to designate qualified entities on an *ad hoc* basis (Article 4).

The Proposal for RAD was further referred to the Council, which in November 2019 adopted its general approach.[133] The Council presented its own vision regarding the legislative framework for collective redress. The main change proposed by the Council was introducing the distinction between domestic and cross-border representative actions. In line with this suggestion, the Member State may decide on the criteria for the designation of qualified entities for domestic representative actions. In contrast, the criteria for the designation of qualified entities for cross-border representative actions would be decided at the EU level. Interestingly, this split of criteria was vigorously

132 European Parliament legislative resolution of 26 March 2019 on the proposal for a directive of the European Parliament and of the Council on representative actions for the protection of the collective interests of consumers and repealing Directive 2009/22/EC, (COM(2018)0184 – C8-0149/2018 – 2018/0089(COD)).

133 Council of the European Union, General approach as of 21 November 2019 on the proposal for a directive of the European Parliament and of the Council on representative actions for the protection of the collective interests of consumers and repealing Directive 2009/22/EC.

defended by the Council, which made it a condition *sine qua non* for giving its green light for the European Commission's Proposal for RAD.

The decision regarding the opt-in or opt-out procedure was left to the discretion of Member States, with a reservation that consumers from another Member State would be required to opt in. Another meaningful change proposed by the Council was to mitigate the effects of the final decision or judgment establishing an infringement. The Council insisted on the solution to which such a ruling shall be treated as evidence—and not a rebuttable presumption—in the context of any other action to seek redress against the same trader for the same practice.

Additionally, the Council discussed the position of the Parliament specified in its resolution. However, to a large degree, the Parliament's suggestions were kept from the Council. Notably, the Council did not include the prohibition of contingency fees and referred to the loser-pays principle and prohibition of punitive damages only in the recitals of the Proposal. This is only one of many examples confirming that the EU institutions have divergent views regarding the shape of the legislative framework for collective redress.

1.6 A critical review of the collective redress framework within RAD

The final shape of the EU collective redress system resulted from political consensus reached at the EU level. It overcame decades of discussions and hesitation about the need and form of collective redress in the EU.[134] RAD leaves significant discretion to the Member States since many issues turned out to be too controversial to regulate them at the EU level. The new legal framework for representative actions requires minimum-level harmonisation and allows Member States to have a higher level of consumer protection.[135] It provides that at least one procedural mechanism that allows qualified entities to bring representative actions in each Member State shall comply with RAD. This mechanism can fit into existing national law or constitute a distinct procedural mechanism.

The following sections will show that the effectiveness of the consumer collective redress system largely relies on Member States making regulatory decisions to meet the obligations outlined in the RAD. The critical areas of effective implementation will include setting down the conditions for domestic actions, national rules on costs, financing collective actions and measures implemented to assist qualified entities, and then bringing representative actions.

134 Biard (2022: 96).
135 Gsell (2021: 1365).

1.6.1 Limits of RAD in light of the principle of procedural autonomy

One reason for the lack of a comprehensive EU-wide regime for collective actions lies in a matter of the principle of procedural autonomy. Under this principle, enforcement of law is left entirely in the hands of Member States.[136] In line with Art. 19 point 1 sentence 2 of the Treaty on the European Union, Member States shall provide remedies sufficient to ensure effective legal protection in the fields covered by EU law. According to procedural autonomy, in case of a lack of relevant rules at the EU level, Member States are free to set up proper procedural mechanisms to enforce EU law.[137] This is also the case of enforcement of EU law on collective redress.[138]

With reference to the principle of procedural autonomy, RAD does not contain provisions on many aspects of proceedings in representative actions. It does not regulate one of the most important issues of collective redress, namely, the requirements for the admissibility of collective actions. Member States have discretion as regards the admissibility criteria as far as national rules do not hamper the effective functioning of the procedural mechanism for representative actions required by the RAD. It is, therefore, for the Member States to decide on the required degree of similarity of individual claims or the minimum number of consumers concerned by a representative action for redress measures in order for the case to be admitted to be heard as a representative action.[139] In line with the principle of non-discrimination, RAD states that the admissibility requirements applicable to specific cross-border representative actions should not differ from those of specific domestic representative actions.

Leaving the admissibility criteria of representative actions at the discretion of the Member States is very risky from the perspective of the goal of RAD. Laying down strict rules on admissibility may hamper the effective functioning of the procedural mechanism for representative action before it even begins. Admissibility criteria assessed by the court always have vast potential for objections and delays since the defendant always contests them in the first place. Moreover, when the admissibility requirements are too general, the judge's attitude towards the collective litigation may be decisive—evidently, some judges are more favourable to representative actions, others might be more reluctant, and some are unfamiliar with this type of proceeding.

It shall also be emphasised that according to RAD, courts or administrative bodies may decide to dismiss manifestly unfounded cases as soon as they receive the necessary information to justify decisions. Such a solution shall

136 Faure, Weber (2017: 823).
137 Krans, Nylund (2020: 1).
138 Weatherill (2022: 112).
139 Rec. 12 of RAD.

prevent abusive litigation, which was feared so much by the business industry. Having in mind that there is no objective evidence of any abusive collective litigation in Europe so far, this relatively low risk is adressed by RAD with exaggeration. It will be up to the national legislator and- in practice- up to national judges or administrative authorities, to decide what constitutes 'the manifestly unfounded claims' and consequently to decide on the number of claims admitted to collective proceedings. Moreover, in the context of third-party funding, discussed below, courts are empowered to take appropriate measures to prevent conflict of interest, such as declaring a specific representative action for redress measure inadmissible. Again, it is difficult to escape the impression that these measures protect business rather than consumer interests, which only supports the strength of the business lobby in enacting RAD.

1.6.2 Choice regarding opt-in or opt-out models

Another vital choice to be made by the Member States in implementing RAD is to decide on the model according to which the group members will be represented. This is somehow suprising having in mind that all empirical evidence confirm that opt-out system is the most effective. RAD refers to opt-in, opt-out and a combination of both systems. In cases of purely domestic representative actions, it leaves the decision about a choice of the system to the discretion of the Member States. However, in the case of representative actions where the consumers affected by infringement do not reside in the Member State of the court or administrative authority before the representative action is brought, RAD imposes the obligation of an opt-in system. In such cases, consumers shall explicitly express their wish to be represented in a representative action to be bound by the judgment. The *ratio legis* of such a solution ensures the sound administration of justice and avoids irreconcilable judgments.

1.6.3 Different requirements for domestic and cross-border representative actions

Conditions of designation and operation of qualified entities are essential for a properly functioning collective redress system. They set procedural guarantees benefitting claimants and defendants in collective actions. They also ensure qualified entities' expertise, independence and capacity in complex mass claims. However, these criteria must be flexible to ensure the effective functioning of the collective redress system. Otherwise, setting too narrow conditions will impede the designation of qualified entities and hinder access to justice. The success of the collective redress system largely depends on which and how many qualified entities are designated domestic and cross-border.

The Commission proposed one set of criteria for qualified entities in the Proposal for RAD. However, in the trialogue process, the Council introduced a distinction between designation criteria for qualified entities authorised to start domestic and cross-border representative actions. Cross-border representative action means a representative action brought by a qualified entity in a Member State other than that in which the qualified entity was designated.[140] Where a qualified entity brings a representative action in the Member State in which it is designated, that representative action should be considered a domestic representative action, even if that action is brought against a trader domiciled in another Member State and even if consumers from several Member States are represented with that representative action.[141] In practice, if a representative action is submitted by a qualified entity from country A against a trader with domicile in country B before a court in country B (according to the general rule of jurisdiction), the case shall be recognised as cross-border representative action. However, suppose a representative action is brought by a representative entity from country B on behalf of consumers from country A, against a trader with domicile in a country B before a court in country B. In that case, the case shall be recognised as a domestic case.

For cross-border representative actions, qualified entities should be subject to the same criteria for designation across the EU, as specified in Article 4 of RAD. Qualified entities must be legally constituted and prove that they had existed for at least 18 months before the designation request. They must demonstrate 12 months of public activity in protecting consumer interests. Member States could allow courts or administrative bodies to reject the legal capacity of a qualified entity designated in another Member State if it is funded by a third party with an economic interest in the outcome of the action.

The criteria mentioned above for qualified entities dealing with cross-border representative actions seem restrictive. It is expected that these requirements will give rise to the potential for objections and delays in the litigation process. The litigation reality shows that if something can be contested in the proceeding, it will be contested. Bearing that cross-border actions for injunctions have rarely been brought up until now, it is likely that adding additional requirements for qualified entities dealing with these cases will decrease the number of cross-border representative actions even more.

We learn from experience that consumer associations in Europe have mainly brought domestic representative actions so far. The best example would be Volkswagen scandal in which collective redress actions had a nearly exclusively domestic nature.[142] Against this background, it seems to be unreasonable that the above-mentioned criteria for qualified entities do not apply

140 Article 3 point 7 of RAD.

141 Rec. 23 of RAD in connection with Article 3 (6).

142 BEUC, Seven years of Dieselgate. A never-ending story, available online at: https://www.beuc.eu/sites/default/files/publications/BEUC-X-2022-130_Dieselgate_7th_report.pdf (access 22.10.2023).

to domestic representative actions. In this respect, Member States can freely establish the requirements for designation under national law. It is worth noting that political concerns dictated such a split of criteria since Member States wanted the EU to refrain from precluding their existing national collective redress procedures.[143]

Another surprising novum introduced to RAD is a prohibition of designating qualified entities dealing with cross-border issues on an *ad hoc* basis (Article 4). As a result, *ad hoc* designation is allowed but only for domestic representative actions. Such a distinction is incomprehensible, especially considering the recent case law that shows that collective actions for investors or financial services users were initiated by foundations established *ad hoc*.[144] It could be expected that this prohibition was also dictated by political considerations and lack of consent of some Member States.

A very interesting solution for the future is the possibility of establishing a European ombudsman dealing with cross-border representative actions for injunctions and redress measures (Article 23(3)). Such an entity could respond to many problems of cross-border collective actions and contribute to the popularisation of this kind of law enforcement. According to RAD, by June 2028 the Commission shall conduct an evaluation report of whether such an entity shall be created.

1.6.4 Lack of private international law rules for representative actions

Regrettably, building on the Proposal, RAD does not establish any rules of private international law regarding representative actions. To achieve this, adopting a regulation (rather than a directive) would be essential. This measure would reduce the chaos by resolving key issues like international jurisdiction and applicable law. Regulation could have also provided a binding effect of the outcome on other consumers harmed by the same infringement and traders infringing the consumer law who were not participating in the proceedings. It will contribute to effective consumer law enforcement.

It has already been pointed out that Regulation 1215/2012[145] does not provide any specific procedures for collective redress. It is justified by the fact that this act was drafted with the tradition of the 'one-on-one' litigation

143 Biard, Voet (2021: 5).

144 Better Finance Legal Committee Position Paper on the Collective Redress Directive, available online at https://betterfinance.eu/wp-content/uploads/CR-Position-Paper.pdf (access 22.10.2023).

145 Regulation (EU) No 1215/2012 of the European Parliament and of the Council of 12 December 2012 on jurisdiction and the recognition and enforcement of judgments in civil and commercial matters (recast), OJEU of 20.12.2012, L 351 p. 1.

model in mind.[146] Legal scholars believe Regulation 1215/2012 needs to be revised for cross-border representative actions.[147] The heated debate on the application of private international law in cases of collective actions[148] was triggered by the CJEU *Schrems* judgment.[149] The case concerned Maximilian Schrems, who started legal proceedings against Facebook before a court in Austria. He alleged that the company infringed on his privacy and data protection rights. Seven other Facebook users, domiciled in Austria and abroad, assigned their claims for allegation of the same infringements to Schrems. One of the questions referred by the Austrian court to CJEU concerned international jurisdiction for disputes concerning consumer contracts where claims have been assigned. The Austrian court asked whether Article 16(1) of Regulation no. 44/2001 (currently Article 18(1) of Regulation no. 1215/2012) can establish additional particular jurisdiction in the domicile of the assignee, thus effectively opening up the possibility of collecting consumer claims from around the world. Schrems argued that establishing such jurisdiction is necessary to answer the need for collective redress and foster effective judicial protection in consumer matters. Neither the CJEU nor the Advocate General shared this view. The CJEU recalled that the consumer forum is applicable only in so far as the consumer is in his capacity as the plaintiff or defendant in proceedings[150] and it does not apply to assigned claims. Consequently, Schrems, who was not a party to the consumer contract in question, cannot enjoy the benefit of the jurisdiction relating to consumer contracts. The CJEU also recalled that the assignment of claims cannot impact the determination of the court having jurisdiction.[151] It shared the Advocate General's opinion that an assignment of claims cannot provide the basis for a new specific forum for a consumer to whom those claims have been assigned.[152]

The argument presented by the CJEU in Schrem's case is compelling. Application of consumer forums to assigned claims will bring a risk of forum shopping by allowing the possibility to choose the place of the more

146 Biard, Voet (2021: 7).

147 *Ibidem.*

148 Pato (2021: 189), Stuerner, Wendelstein (2018: 1091), Modrzejewski (2018: 80–88), Mucha (2022: 52).

149 CJEU judgment as of 25.01.2018, C-498/16, *Maximilian Schrems v. Facebook Ireland Limited*, ECLI:EU:C:2018:37.

150 CJEU judgment as of 19.01.1993, C-89/91, *Shearson Lehman Hutton Inc. v. TVB Treuhandgesellschaft für Vermögensverwaltung und Beteiligungen mbH.*, ECLI:EU:C:1993:15.

151 CJEU judgment as of 18.07.2013, C-147/12, *ÖFAB, Östergötlands Fastigheter AB v. Frank Koot and Evergreen Investments BV*, ECLI: EU:C:2013:490; CJEU judgment as of 21.05.2015, C-352/13, Cartel Damage Claims Hydrogen Peroxide SA (CDC) v. Akzo Nobel NV I in., ECLI:EU:C:2015:335.

152 CJEU judgment, C-498/16, *Schrems*, para. 48.

favourable courts for collective actions.[153] In the Attorney General's words, such a solution could lead to unrestrained targeted assignment to consumers in any jurisdiction with more favourable case law, reduced costs, or more generous jurisdictional aid, potentially leading to the overburdening of some jurisdictions.[154] Although Regulation 44/2001 does not establish a new particular jurisdiction, Attorney Generals saw the possibility of establishing such jurisdiction in the national law.[155]

Regrettably, RAD did not introduce any consumer forum rule concerning cross-border representative actions. The lack of such regulation implies that the general rule on jurisdiction applies. Namely, the defendant is sued in the Member State of his domicile. In cross-border representative actions, the old problems under Directive 2009/22/EC (costs, lack of qualified entities' expertise in foreign law) still need to be solved. The qualified entity from the consumers' Member States is still obliged to start the proceedings in a different Member State.

1.6.5 Unsolved problem of funding and costs of proceedings

Adequate funding is key to a successful collective redress system.[156] Because most consumer organisations and foundations acting as representative entities of non-profit-making character have very limited financial resources and public funding is often insufficient, an alternative funding source is essential for collective litigation. Without adequate resources to cover all the costs of proceedings, such as court fees, lawyer fees, expert fees and administrative costs entailed by the need to inform the consumers at all stages of the proceedings properly, qualified entities may be deterred from bringing representative actions and access to justice may be hindered.[157]

Despite the above, European legislators remain sceptical of third-party funding and favour entities with public support. A final version of RAD allows third-party funding only insofar as it is allowed by the national law of Member States and only insofar as some safeguards preventing conflicts of interests are provided.[158] For this purpose, the decisions of qualified entities shall not be unduly influenced by a third-party funder in a manner that would be detrimental to the consumers concerned. At this point, it is worth discussing the conflicts of interest. RAD specifies that conflicts of interest can be implied by the direct

153 Pato (2021: 189), Stuerner, Wendelstein (2018: 1091).
154 Opinion of the Advocate General, case C-498/16 *Schrems*, ECLI:EU:C:2017:863, para 105.
155 Opinion of the Advocate General, case C-498/16, *Schrems*, para 117.
156 Kramer, Tillema (2020: 165–181).
157 European Commission, *Thematic debate on funding of actions and public assistance to qualified entities*, available online at: https://commission.europa.eu/system/files/2022-09/1_3_197467_discussion_paper_2_rad_workshop.pdf (access 10.10.2023).
158 Stadler (2022: 153).

funding of an action by a trader who operates in the same market as the defendant, thus being the defendant's competitor and possibly having an economic interest in the outcome of the representative action. However, the European Commission interprets this provision by allowing the indirect funding of representative action by organisations financed through equal contributions by their members or through donations, including traders' donations in the framework of corporate social responsibility initiatives or crowdfunding. These contributions should be considered eligible for third-party funding, provided that the third-party funding complies with the requirements of transparency, independence and the absence of conflicts of interest. However, as mentioned above, Member States can decide whether they allow third-party funding.

To assess compliance with general rules regarding finding representative actions, national courts and administrative entities are empowered to take many actions. In order to prove compliance with the requirement of transparency, qualified entities shall disclose to the court or administrative authorities a financial overview that lists the sources of funds used to support the representative actions. Further, courts or administrative authorities are empowered to require the qualified entity to refuse or make changes regarding relevant funding and, if necessary, to reject the legal standing of the qualified entity in a specific representative action.

In theory, qualified entities could turn to commercial litigation funders to finance the representative actions. However, leaving the decision about third-party funding to the discretion of the Member States deprives many qualified entities of this kind of funding in practice. It is unlikely for those Member States that do not allow third-party funding to change their legislative landscape in this regard in the implementation of RAD. Even with this, Member States must ensure that qualified entities are not prevented by the costs of proceedings from seeking effective injunctive and or redress measures, Article 20(1), but at the same time, they are not obliged to finance representative actions by any means. Some national legal orders provide measures that address the challenges posed by the costs of proceedings such as structural public support, exceptions from court fees, access to legal aid, etc. However, experience shows that more than these measures is needed to satisfy the principle of effectiveness of the collective redress system. Indeed, collective actions are very complicated and extremely expensive. Therefore, only private investors with an economic interest in bringing the representative action (as an investment with the agreed rate of return) can genuinely meet the needs of funding collective litigation.

1.7 Conclusion

The road to European collective redress has been long and twisted. Despite more than 30 years of discussion and debate, the EU has not enacted a free-standing collective redress regime, since most of the key decisions are left at the discrecion of the Member States The legislative framework provided by RAD sought to find a balance between consumer access to justice and safeguards to avoid abusive litigation. However, it is difficult to escape the impression that protection of business industry, and not consumers, is at the heart of this legislative framework.

The existing framework is significantly limited by the principle of procedural autonomy. According to RAD, each Member State shall have at least one procedural mechanism to allow bringing representative actions but it is up to the Member States to create the procedural rules governing this matter. The main success at the EU level remains the creation of a mechanism for collective redress that includes both injunctive and compensatory measures. There is little doubt that consumers would seek compensation collectively. But, in order to make it happen, some additional actions must be undertaken by the Member States.

Funding the collective redress is the most basic need that must be satisfied by Member States to fully implement RAD. In recognition that consumers should not bear the costs of the proceedings on one hand, and having in mind that the EU collective regime should not be based on the activity of profit-driven lawyers on the other, there emerges a question of who shall pay for representative actions in the EU. RAD is very vague in this respect. One possible answer is allowing public funds for representative entities. Currently consumer organisations in many Member States are underfunded and there is no sign of any change despite implementation of RAD. To this end, third-party funding is promising. One may say that, contrary to the Commission's claims, inflow of third-party capital will bring 'representative actions' in a 'European way' somehow closer to the US class action style in the sense that the proceedings might be financed by the business sector. In the absence of provisions regarding third-party funding in many Member States, it is expected that the question of the control of the source of the funds will be regulated in more detail. This would be indispensable in order to prevent third-party traders from providing financing for collective actions against their competitors or dependent entities, as stipulated by RAD.

The success of the representative actions in Europe is also controlled by judges and/or administrative bodies adjudicating and deciding on collective actions. These proceedings are new to most EU Member States' legal systems. Even in those Member States (or former Member States in the case of the UK), where some forms of collective redress existed before the implementation of RAD (such as Belgium or Poland) national experiences are not very broad. It is not surprising, since in the EU there is generally no class action culture. Continental law judges are mostly reluctant towards collective action because they are simply unfamiliar with this kind of proceedings. It is easier for them to adjudicate in the cases brought as a result of the individual proceedings, which they are used to doing on a daily basis. For the representative actions to be effective, the judges and administrative authorities must be convinced through education that this kind of proceeding can help to improve the functioning of the justice system by providing broader redress to more persons harmed by law-breaking traders. Thus, judges shall consider collective actions as a mechanism that could minimise their workload rather than as a mechanism that adds them some additional tasks. For those judges and administrative authorities who want to 'cooperate for the good functioning of representative actions across the EU,' the European Commission created the electronic platform 'EC-React' for information exchange on representative actions across the EU. However, registration on the platform is on a voluntarily basis, so again, there must be the will of the judges and administrative bodies to share their know-how and build a community that will help to develop and familiarise collective litigation in the EU.

A vital issue that must be duly analyzed by the Member States is the involvement of lawyers in the representative actions. Unsurprisingly, RAD does not mention this question at all. It provides that the representative actions must be brought by representative entities but it remains doubtful whether it could be done properly without the support of lawyers. Having in mind that collective actions are time-consuming and costly, the important issue remains the lawyer's remunerations. Except in occasional *pro bono* cases, one shall not expect that law firms will represent consumers for free. The possible solution could be an introduction of contingency fees, which is currently not regulated under RAD. It can be assumed that since it is not clearly prohibited by RAD, Member States may decide upon allowing fees for lawyers that are paid only if a case is won. It would be reasonable to expect that the Member States will regulate the amount of fees, which could encourage law firms to represent the consumer organisations and make the representative actions profitable, on the one hand, and will guarantee that consumers will not be deprived from the significant amount of compensation awarded by the court or administrative authority, on the other.

Despite the many problems arising out of the application of Directive 2009/22/EC (being currently repealed by RAD) caused by its vagueness, these issues were not addressed by the EU in the new legislation. The length and costs of proceedings, difficulties relating to cross-border proceedings—these are just some examples from the long list of issues that were very well known to the EU legislator but regrettably not addressed by RAD. The wide margin of appreciation left to Member States has been criticised already in relation to the safeguards contained in Recommendation 2013/396/EU, which allowed many exemptions for Member States. This margin was considered the reason this soft law mechanism was unsuccessful.

Instead of learning from the mistakes of the past, the EU is stubbornly following the same path. Perhaps the most striking example is that RAD leaves the choice to the Member States as regards the system of consumers joining a collective action. RAD does not specify whether it should be the opt-in, opt-out, or a mixed system. Leaving this crucial point to the discretion of Member States excludes the possibility of the creation of a coherent system of collective redress at the EU level. This—in turn—may bring some doubts regarding the enforcement of redress measures and injunctive orders issued in the course of injunction proceedings at the EU level. To be sure, better coherence brings better enforcement of the law. However, it may be argued that instead of specific solutions in this respect, the EU institutions should go further than issuing vague declarations. Keeping in mind all of the above mentioned, it will be up to the Member States to decide whether RAD will significantly improve the European landscape of collective redress and strengthen the mechanism for the protection of collective consumer interests.

References

Amaro R, Azar-Baud M J, Corneloup S, Fauvarque-Cosson B, Jault-Seseke F (2018) *Collective redress in the Member States of the European Union.* Study commissioned by the European Parliament.

Baker L, Perino A, Silver C (2015) Is the price right? Study of fee-setting in securities class action, *Columbia Law Review*, Vol. 115(6) , pp.1371-1451.

Biard A (2018) Collective redress in the EU: A rainbow behind the clouds, *ERA Forum*, Vol. 19, pp. 189–204.

Biard A (2022) *'Je t'aime moi non plus'*: Why Europe needs strong collective redress, In: Kramer X et al (eds), *Delivering justice: A holistic and multidisciplinary approach. Liber amicorum in honour of Christopher Hodges*, Hart, pp. 87–100.

Biard A, Voet S (2021) Collective redress in the EU: Will it finally come true? In: Uzelac A, Voet S (eds), *Class actions in Europe: Holy grail or a wrong trail*, Springer, pp. 287–299.

Durovic M, Micklitz H (2017) *Internationalization of consumer law: A game changer*, Springer.

Eisenberg T, Miller G (2003) *What is a reasonable attorney fee? An empirical study of class action settlements*, Cornell Law Faculty Publications, Paper 354 (electronic resource).

Ervo L (2015) Opt-in is out, and opt-out is in: Dimensions based on the nordic options and the commission's recommendation, In: Hess B et al (eds), *EU civil justice: Current issues and future outlook*, Hart Publishing, 2015, pp. 167–200.

Faure M, Weber F (2017) The diversity of the EU approach to law enforcement – towards a coherent model inspired by a law and economics approach, *German Law Review,* Vol. 4, pp. 823–880.

Gsell B (2021) The new European directive on representative actions for the protection of the collective interests of consumers- a huge but blurry step forward? *Common Market Law Review*, Vol. 58, pp. 1365–1400.

Hamulakowa K (2018) Opt-out systems in collective redress. EU perspectives and the present situation in Czech Republik, *Hungarian Journal of Legal Studies,* Vol. 59 (1), pp. 95–117.

Hensler D (2011) The future of mass litigation: Global class actions and third party litigation funding, *The George Washington Law Review*, Vol. 79(2), pp. 306–323.

Hensler D (2016) Can private class actions enforce regulations? Do they? Should they? In: Bignami F, Zaring D (eds), *Comparative law and regulation: Understanding the global regulatory process*, Edgar Elgar, pp. 238–272.

Hensler D et al (2021) *The globalization of mass civil litigation: Lessons from the Volkswagen "Clean Diesel" case*, Rand Corporation.

Hodges C (2014) Collective redress: A breakthrough or a Damp Squibb? *Journal of Consumer Policy*, Vol. 37, pp. 67–89.

Hodges C, Voet S (2018) *Delivering collective redress: New technologies*, Hart.

Howells G (2017) EU consumer access to justice and enforcement, In: Howells G, Twigg-Flesner C, Wilhelmsson T (eds), *Rethinking EU consumer law*, Routledge (electronic resource).

Ioannidou M (2011) Enhancing the consumer's role in EU private competition law enforcement: A normative and practical approach, *The Competition Law Review*, Vol. 8(1), pp. 59–85.

Jabłonowska A, Namysłowska M (2018) Nowy ład konsumentów? O planowanych zmianach prawa konsumenckiego w Unii Europejskiej, *Europejski Przegląd Sądowy*, Vol. 10, pp. 11–17.

Keirsblick B (2013) The *erga omnes* effect of the finding of an unfair contract term: Nemezi, *Common Market Law Review*, Vol. 50(5), pp. 1467–1478.

Klonoff R (2018) Application of the new "proportionality" discovery rule in class actions: Much ado about nothing, *Vanderbilt Law Review*, Vol. 71 (6), pp.1949–1991.

Kowalczyk-Zagaj A (2018) Przegląd najważniejszych propozycji legislacyjnych Komisji Europejskiej w "Nowym ładzie dla konsumentów", *internetowy Kwartalnik Antymonopolowy i Regulacyjny*, Vol. 6(7), pp. 119–131.

Kramer X, Tillema I (2020) The funding of collective redress by entrepreneurial parties: The EU and Dutch context, *Revista Ítalo-Española de Derecho Procesal*, Vol. 2, pp. 165–181.

Krans A, Nylund A (2020) Aspects of procedural autonomy, In: Krans B, Nylund A (eds), *Procedural autonomy across Europe*, Intersentia, pp. 1–12.

Luzak J (2017) You too will be judged: erga omnes effect of registered unfair contract terms in Poland, *Journal of European Consumer and Market Law*, Vol. 3, pp. 120-124.

Miller A (2018) The American class action: From birth to maturity, *Theoretical Inquiries in Law*, Vol. 19 (1), pp. 1–45.

Modrzejewski P (2018) Problem utraty statusu konsumenta korzystającego z portali społecznościowych, *Glosa*, Vol. 3, pp. 80–88.

Money-Kyrle R (2016) Legal standing in collective redress actions for breach of EU rights: Facilitating or frustrating common standards and access to justice? In Hess B, Bergstrom M, Storskrubb E (eds), *EU civil justice: Current issues and future outlook*, Hart, pp. 223–256.

Mucha J (2019b) Heading towards an effective mechanism for the protection of collective interests of consumers – some comments on the proposal for a directive on representative actions, *Yearbook of Antitrust and Regulatory Studies*, Vol. 12, pp. 205–230.

Mucha J (2022) Prawo konsumenckie Unii Europejskiej – pojęcie konsumenta w ujęciu dynamicznym oraz cesja roszczeń konsumenckich – wprowadzenie i wyrok Trybunału Sprawiedliwości z 25.01.2018 r., C-498/16, Maximilian Schrems przeciwko Facebook Ireland Limited, *Europejski Przegląd Sądowy,* Vol. 1, pp. 52–60.

Nagy C (2019) *Collective actions in Europe: A comparative economic and transsystemic analysis*, Springer.

Namysłowska M (2017) Erga-Omnes Wirkung von missbraeuchlichen AGB in einem oeffentlichen Register, *Europaeisches Zeitschrift fuer Wirtschaftsrecht*, Vol.5, pp. 194-195.

Oleksiewicz I (2012) *Dyrektywa Parlamentu Europejskiego i Rady 2009/22/WE z dnia 23 kwietnia 2009 r. w sprawie nakazów zaprzestania szkodliwych praktyk w celu ochrony interesów konsumentów. Komentarz*, Lexis Nexis.

Pato A (2021) *Jurisdiction and cross-border collective redress: A European private international law perspective*, Hart.

Piszcz A (2017) Compensatory collective redress: will it be part of private enforcement of competition law in CEE countries? *Yearbook of Antitrust and Regulatory Studies*, Vol. 10(15), pp. 223–250.

Sahin E (2019) *Collective redress and EU competition law*, Routledge.

Sieradzka M (2008) Komentarz do dyrektywy 98/27/WE w sprawie nakazów zaprzestania szkodliwych praktyk w celu ochrony interesów konsumentów, In: Sieradzka M (ed), *Ustawa o ochronie konkurencji i konsumentów. Komentarz*, LEX (electronic source).

Sorabji J (2014) Reflections on the commission communication on collective redress, *Irish Journal of European Law*, Vol. 17(1), pp. 62–76.

Stadler A (2013) The commission's recommendation on common principles of collective redress and private international law issues, *Nederlands International Privatrecht*, Vol. 4, pp. 483–488.

Stadler A (2021) *Are class actions finally (re) conquering Europe?* Iuridica International.

Stadler A (2022) Third-party funding in collective redress In: Kramer X et al (eds), *Delivering justice: A holistic and multidisciplinary approach: Liber amicorum in honour of Christopher Hodges*, Hart, pp. 151–160.

Stadler A et al (2020) *Collective and mass litigation in Europe: Model rules for effective dispute resolution*, Edward Elgar.

Stuerner M, Wendelstein C (2018) Datenschutzrechtliche „Sammelklagen" im Zuständigkeitsregime der Brüssel Ia-VO, *Juristen Zeitung*, Vol. 22, pp. 1083–1092.

Vanleenhove C (2017) *Punitive damages in private international law: Lessons for the European Union*, Cambridge University Press.

Visscher L, Faure M (2021) A law and economics perspective on the EU directive on representative actions, *Journal of Consumer Policy,* Vol. 44, pp. 455–482.

Voet S (2014) European collective redress: A status quaestionis, *International Journal of Procedural Law*, Vol. 4(1), pp. 79–128.

Weatheril S (2022) Collective redress in EU consumer law: How it is, how it could be In: Kramer X et al (eds), *Delivering justice: A holistic and multidisciplinary approach: Liber amicorum in honour of Christopher Hodges*, Hart, pp. 101–118.

Wyżykowski B (2018) Skuteczna ochrona konsumentów a gwarancje procesowe przedsiębiorców. Glosa do wyroku TS z 21 grudnia 2016 r. w sprawie C-119/15 Biuro podróży Partner sp. z o.o. sp. k przeciwko w Dąbrowie Górniczej przeciwko Prezesowi Urzędu Ochrony Konkurencji i Konsumentów, *internetowy Kwartalnik Antymonopolowy i Regulacyjny*, Vol. 4(7), pp. 107–122.

2 Private enforcement of consumer collective interests

A comparative perspective

In the EU, there is no unified system for law enforcement. Instead, Member States defer to the national legislatures to decide how consumer rights will be effectively enforced in particular jurisdictions. EU law requires the collaboration of the Member States to implement and transpose European legislation into national law and to enforce the relevant provisions. Due to the difficulties that Member States encounter with regard to the choice of procedural options, an implementation deficit may occur in many areas, including consumer law.[1]

National traditions in the domain of consumer law enforcement are varied. Some Member States traditionally followed private enforcement while others adopted a public law enforcement model (most Central and Eastern European countries, which, within the process of accession to the EU, were obliged to establish a public authority with general and horizontal competence regarding consumer affairs). While the essential function of public enforcement of the law is deterrence from its infringements, the main focus of private enforcement is on compensation and redress to harmed consumers.[2] However, with the rise of the global economy, the traditional classification and division of public and private enforcement is becoming outdated. It is argued that a more complex approach is needed to provide for redress of mass harms[3] and enforcement of consumer law shall be currently regarded as a mix of public and private methods.[4]

In Chapter 1 it was explained that the term 'collective redress' refers to a wide range of procedural mechanisms enabling the enforcement of collective consumer interests. Although these mechanisms are very diverse—collective redress models and types differ significantly worldwide—they serve the same purpose, namely to enable a large number of individuals to seek redress in one proceedings.[5] The national laws of the Member States provide a variety of legal means to enforce consumer rights, which can be performed either within

1 Faure, Weber (2017: 823, 826).
2 Piszcz (2017: 223, 242).
3 Voet, Dethier (2024: 13).
4 Riefa, Saintier (2021: 2).
5 Amaro et al (2018: 13-14)

DOI: 10.4324/9781003520849-3

the framework of judicial, administrative, or mixed paths.[6] The proceedings can be initiated by private entities (the group of consumers or representative entities) or public enforcers such as governmental administrative bodies, public regulators, or ombudsmen. As a result, consumer law enforcement in the EU is very heterogeneous.

It follows from the considerations included in Chapter 1 that the legislative framework stipulated in Directive 2020/1828 on Representative Actions (RAD)[7] did not constitute the free-standing regime for collective redress in the EU. RAD delegates to the Member States discretion in designing the mechanism for representative actions either as a part of an existing or new system for collective injunctive or redress measures or both.[8] In line with the principle of procedural autonomy, RAD does not contain provisions on the details of proceedings involving representative actions. Instead, it directs Member States to promulgate rules on such things as admissibility, evidence, or the means of appeal applicable to representative actions. Additionally, Member States have the authority to decide whether a representative action can be brought in judicial proceedings, administrative proceedings, or both, depending on the area of law or the type of economic sector.

Chapter 2 discusses the private enforcement of consumer collective interests in the three European jurisdictions that are considered to be the most relevant in this field.[9] It focuses on the various legal mechanisms that function in the Member States and the UK, serving the consumers as a means of collective redress. The main analysis focuses on the legal solutions adopted in Belgium (2.1), the Netherlands (2.2), as well as England and Wales (2.3). It includes changes introduced to the national laws by the implementation of RAD. The goal of this chapter is to indicate how these mechanisms operate in practice and which solutions are worth reception on the grounds of Polish law by way of good practice.

2.1 Belgium[10]

The first national legislation chosen for scrutinising in terms of private enforcement of consumer collective interests is Belgian legislation. It is

6 Azar-Baud et al (2024:7)

7 Directive (EU) 2020/1828 of the European Parliament and of the Council of 25 November 2020 on representative actions for the protection of the collective interests of consumers and repealing Directive 2009/22/EC, OJEU of 4.12.2020 No. L 409 p.1 ("RAD").

8 For the status of implementation of RAD across Member States see: Steennot (2024: 185), Stein (2024: 211), Biard (2024: 231), Rott (2024: 255), Howells (2024: 277), Bugatti (2024: 289), Weber (2024: 313).

9 Over past five years, the UK and the Netherlands have the highest number of class actions in Europe, see: CMS European class action report (2023:electronic source).

10 This section builds on the research findings drawing from the author's publication: Mucha (2019).

worth examining for at least three reasons. First, the Belgian class action system has been in effect for a decade. In contrast to other EU Member States, Belgium has considerable experience in the use of the class action mechanism. Secondly, Belgian law demonstrated flexibility in the use of the opt-in and opt-out models. At the first negotiation phase of proceedings, parties may decide which model they prefer. Until 2024, with some limits, Belgian courts were authorised to decide whether to choose opt-in or opt-out in case of lack of settlement of the parties. After RAD was implemented, the mandatory opt-in system was imposed if the settlement is not reached and a claim is confirmed admissible by the court. Third, Belgian law favours the out-of-court dispute resolution of mass harm. It is possible to reach settlement before the proceedings, during the mandatory negotiation phase after the class is certified, and during the procedure of the merits of the case.[11]

As the course of the collective proceedings under Belgian law has already been extensively covered in other studies,[12] it does not need to be revisited in detail here. However, to guide further discussion, the following section provides a brief account of some highlights of the Belgian system of collective enforcement of consumer rights with a focus on the latest legislative changes introduced as a result of the implementation of RAD. Furthermore, examining examples of past class actions reveals both the achievements and limitations of the system of collective redress in Belgium.

2.1.1 Actions for collective redress under the Belgian Code of Economic Law

Belgium's consumer collective redress mechanism was introduced in 2014. It is based on representative action, which is similar to the model introduced recently at the EU level by RAD. Book XVII of the Belgian Code of Economic Law (CEL) provides for the procedural instrument called 'an action for collective redress.' Such action can be submitted on behalf of the group of consumers or, since June 2018, by small and medium-sized enterprises (SMEs) by a class representative. To represent the group, the class representative does not need any prior authorisation from the members of the class. The class action proceedings can be commenced before the Commercial Court of Brussels (before 2018 also before the court of the first instance) and the judgment can be appealed against at the Brussels Court of Appeal.

Before the implementation of RAD, the class representative must have fulfiled specific criteria designated by CEL. It must have been either: (i) a consumer protection organisation, (ii) a non-profit organisation that satisfies

11 Voet (2021: 136).
12 Nowak (2021: 192); Voet (2021: 137).

certain legal criteria, (iii) a Consumer Ombudsman Service[13] (only representing the group in the stage of negotiation of an agreement on collective redress), or (iv) a representative body recognised by the Member State of the EU or the European Economic Area (EEA) to act as a representative according to the Commission's recommendation on collective redress. In the case of SMEs, the class representative must be either (i) an interprofessional organisation with legal personality that defends the interest of SMEs, (ii) a non-profit organisation with a legal personality whose corporate purpose is directly connected to the collective damage suffered by the group, or (iii) a representative body recognised by the Member State of the EU or the EEA mentioned above in terms of consumer claims.

In 2024, after the implementation of RAD, standing was expanded to cover qualified entities that are recognised by the Minister of Economic Affairs, who checks whether all requirements set forth in RAD are met.[14] The requirements are identical for the purpose of bringing domestic and cross-border representative actions. Further, the collective actions can also be brought by qualified entities from other Member States and, notably, domestic actions by entities that are designated by the court as qualified entities on an *ad hoc* basis. The Consumer Ombudsman Service remains entitled in terms of negotiating settlements only.

The precise enumeration of the specific categories of the entities entitled to bring representative actions serves the purpose of ameliorating frivolous or abusive litigation, which could occur if the group of eligible entities was more broadly defined.[15] As a further safeguard, litigation against the traders may be bought only as a result of the violation of its contractual obligations or an infringement of rights granted to the consumers or SMEs by the European or Belgian regulations or acts that are enumerated in Article XVII.37 CEL.[16]

The Belgian class action process consists of four phases: the admissibility (certification) phase, the compulsory negotiation phase, the litigation phase and the pay-out (enforcement) phase.

Until 2024, the admissibility (certification) phase was required to have been completed within two months after bringing an action. In practice, however, the process was much longer. Once RAD was implemented in Belgium, a more realistic time frame was introduced. Currently, the court is required to decide on the admissibility of the claim within six months. During this phase the court is verifying admissibility criteria: primarily whether a possible

13 "Consumer Ombudsman Service" is sometimes translated also as a "Consumer Mediation Service".

14 Article 4.3. of RAD.

15 Boularbah, van den Bossche (2018: 21).

16 For details on infringements for which collective redress in possible in Belgium see: Steennot (2024: 192–193).

infringement of the law by the trader falls into the scope of class action and whether the class action is superior to an individual claim. The second criterion is considered discretionary.[17] There are some elements that can be taken into consideration by the judge (such as the potential size of the group, the existence of individual damage that is sufficiently related to the collective damage, the complexity and legal efficiency of the action of collective redress), but they are of a very broad nature. Before RAD was implemented in Belgium, the court also verified whether the representative entity satisfied the statutory requirements, including adequacy. Under the new law, this requirement does not apply anymore as all qualified entities need to be screened in advance in order to be recognised by the Minister of Economic Affairs.

The second phase is the compulsory negotiation phase, which lasts from three to six months after certification. At this stage parties may decide whether they prefer the opt-in or opt-out model. If the collective settlement is reached, the parties submit the proposed agreement to the court for approval. The court can refuse approval only if (i) the settlement provides a remedy that is manifestly unfair, (ii) the opt-in or opt-out period agreed upon by the parties is manifestly unfair, (iii) the proposed settlement provides for manifestly unreasonable additional publication measures, or (iv) it awards the compensation to the class representative that exceeds its actual costs. Additionally, the settlement would be refused if it violates public policy or it is unenforceable. The settlement must be published in the official journal and on the website of the Belgian Ministry of Economic Affairs. If the trader has a list of persons harmed or can easily compile such list, it is obliged to contact these consumers directly at its own expense.

Under the old system, in case of a lack of agreement reached at the negotiation stage of proceedings, the court decided between the opt-in or opt-out system. The opt-in model was mandatory if any physical or moral damages were claimed for the consumers who do not reside in Belgium or for SMEs that do not have their main establishment in Belgium. Currently, in the event the parties do not reach an agreement, Belgian law provides a unique mechanism called 'late opt-in.' This approach makes it possible for consumers to join the group once the liability of the trader is established. Consumers are required to join the group within four months of the publication of the court's decision on the trader's liability.

In the event of a settlement impasse, the litigation phase commences. The court adjudicates the merits of the case. Secondly, the court determines the appropriate remedy. The main principle in terms of damages is the principle of full compensation, while punitive damages are not allowed. Under Belgian law, contingency fees are prohibited, which means that in practice the class representative (qualified entity) assumes the risk of bearing the costs, which

17 Hodges, Voet (2018: 45).

cannot be recovered if the case is deemed inadmissible, if no settlement is reached, or if the trader wins the case. Although third-party funding is not directly prohibited by the law, there is no experience with third-party funding in Belgium to date.

The last phase, pay-out (enforcement), concerns the distribution of compensation (if such was awarded). The court appoints the claim administrator/settler who oversees the enforcement of the decision or settlement and provides a report to the court. The claim administrator/settler provides the list of the consumers included in the group to the trader and to the court. In case of dispute as to the group composition, the court makes the determination.

2.1.2 Actions for collective redress in practice—case studies

Starting from 2014, when consumer class actions were introduced in Belgium, ten class action claims have been brought before the court for the protection of the collective interest of consumers.[18] The majority of the representative actions (nine out of ten) were brought by the Belgian non-profit consumer organisation Testachats,[19] which in all of the cases was found by the court to be adequate to initiate the proceedings. As of the date of this book, only one case was brought by another authority—the Belgian Consumer Mediation Service[20]—and its standing was questionable by the court. As the opt-out model was generally considered the most effective, it is not surprising that in all cases consumer organisations asked the court for this type of group participation. All of the cases were governed by the old law (before the implementation of RAD in Belgium). Five representative actions, initiated by Testachats, were already discussed in the literature of the subject.[21] In order not to repeat these findings, in what follows only the most recent cases will be presented.

18 There was also one case initiated for the benefit of SMEs by the Brussels Hotel and Catering Federation and the Neutral Syndicate for the Self-Employed against the Belgian association for authors, composers and publishers, as they were required to continue paying licensing fees during COVID-19 lockdowns despite bars and restaurants being forced to close. According to publicly available information, a settlement was reached in this case, granting hospitality operators a 75% discount on one of their following month's bills, see: Amaury Michaux, "Handelszaken krijgen extra korting van Sabam", Brussel, Het Nieuwsblad, 16.01.2023.+

19 https://www.test-achats.be/ (access 10.10.2023). The Author would like to thank Jean-Philippe Ducart from Testachats for his great help in identifying representative actions brought by Testachats in Belgium.

20 https://consumerombudsman.be/en (access 10.10.2023).

21 Hodges, Voet (2018: 46–48). The five class actions discussed by these authors were brought by Testachats against: (i) Thomas Cook Airlines Belgium (air passenger rights), (ii) SNCB/NMBS National Railway Company in Belgium (rail passenger rights), (iii) Proximus Telecom Operator (decoders telecom), (iv) Volkswagen, and (v) five companies illegally reselling concert tickets.

2.1.2.1 *The Groupon (Luierbox)* case

The first case discussed here will be regarded as a consumer success story. A representative action was brought against Groupon—the website service that offers virtual coupons for deals on various products and services. One of Groupon's partners includes Luierbox, a company that offers its customers a subscription to a monthly delivery of diapers for EUR 300 or EUR 350. It turned out, however, that the product was never delivered to subscribers.[22] Almost 1,200 consumers were involved. Groupon refused to give a refund to the customers as it considered itself as an intermediary only. As a consequence, Testachats brought a claim to initiate the class action proceedings before the court of the first instance in October 2017. In August 2018, which was still before the admissibility phase of the proceedings, Testachats signed an agreement with Groupon in Luierbox.[23] As a result, the proceedings did not reach the certification decision. This amicable solution allowed consumers to obtain a refund in the amount of EUR 200 in cash and EUR 100 in the form of credit on the customer's Groupon account.[24] This case exemplifies the deterrent effect of the representative action mechanism—it proves that no full class action proceedings was needed because the case was settled. Some companies infringing consumer rights can be motivated to pay damages by the mere act of submitting action to court (even when the case has not been certified by the court).

2.1.2.2 *The Facebook* case

The only class action related to data protection breach so far in Belgium was the case initiated against Facebook as a consequence of the Facebook-Cambridge Analytica scandal, revealed in March 2018.[25] It was reported that Cambridge Analytica, a company that specialises in psychological profiling, harvested the personal data of Facebook users without their consent and passed it on for political advertising purposes. As a result, four European consumer organisations, Testachats in Belgium, OCU in Spain, Deco Proteste in Portugal and Altroconsumo in Italy, started a campaign called 'My Data Is Mine,' making consumers aware of the violation of their rights by Facebook.[26] The Cambridge Analytica scandal gave rise to the proceedings for unfair

22 Testachats: https://www.test-achats.be/famille-prive/jeunes-parents/news/grouponluierbox (access 10.10.2023).

23 Testachats: https://www.test-achats.be/actions-collectives/action-collective-groupon-compensation (access 10.10.2023).

24 Testachats: https://www.test-achats.be/actions-collectives/action-collective-groupon-compensation (access 10.10.2023).

25 Inga (2024: 5)

26 My Data is Mine campaign: https://www.mydataismine.com/ (access 10.10.2023).

commercial practices. In September 2018, the UK Information Commissioner's Office fined Facebook GBP 500,000 for both lack of transparency and failing to protect user's information.[27] Similarly, the Italian Competition Authority confirmed misuse of data by the social network and in December 2018 ordered Facebook to pay EUR 10 million for unfair commercial practices using user data for commercial practices.[28]

After unsuccessful negotiations with Facebook, the above-mentioned consumer organisations launched collective actions in each country.[29] In May 2018, Testachats initiated collective action against Facebook before the Commercial Court in Brussels; 42,281 people registered for the class action to claim compensation of EUR 200 each for the misuse of the data. The class action ended in April 2021 without any court decision on the merits of the lawsuit. Facebook and Testachats announced an agreement providing 'a three-year collaboration to improve consumer digital lives and create added value for them.'[30] As a result of the settlement, the parties agreed to implement several initiatives that focus on sustainability, online scams and digital empowerment. Unfortunately, Facebook did not pay any direct compensation to the consumers.[31]

2.1.2.3 *The energy suppliers* case

The case against energy suppliers is unique because it was initiated by a member of the Belgian Consumer Ombudsman Service (and not by the leading consumer organisation, Testachats). This authority is competent to issue such proceedings only to reach a collective settlement, so the class action cannot lead to a decision on the merits or to the payment of compensation. The proceeding was also novel because, for the first time, a complaint had been brought not only by consumers but also by small and medium-sized enterprises.

27 The Guardian: https://www.theguardian.com/technology/2018/oct/25/facebook-fined-uk-privacy-access-user-data-cambridge-analytica (access 10.10.2023).

28 The Guardian: https://www.theguardian.com/technology/2018/dec/07/italian-regulator-fines-facebook-89m-for-misleading-users(access 10.10.2023).

29 BEUC: The Guardian: https://www.beuc.eu/press-media/news-events/euroconsumers-launch-collective-action-against-facebook; https://www.consumersinternational.org/news-resources/blog/posts/not-your-puppets-euroconsumers-interview/ (access 10.10.2023).

30 Facebook press release: https://assets.ctfassets.net/iapmw8ie3ije/1sxhDq70DZNeZgPR3jsXjz/35bf318dca775644f2b725d118774939/Joint_press_release_with_Facebook.pdf (access 10.10.2023).

31 Politico: https://www.politico.eu/article/eu-lawsuit-against-facebook-partnership-euroconsumers-complainants/ (access 10.10.2023).

In September 2018, the Belgian Energy Ombudsman, one of the members of the Belgian Consumer Ombudsman Services,[32] initiated a class action against several energy suppliers (electricity or natural gas) before the Brussels Commercial Court. It disputed the legality of a fixed amount of fees charged by energy suppliers for an entire year's supply in the case when the customer terminated the energy contract earlier in the year. The fees amounted to EUR 60 or more per energy source for a full year. In its press release, the Energy Ombudsman stated that it received over 300 complaints from customers affected by this practice, however, it estimated that the number of the customers concerned is over 40,000 and the total financial compensation of the collective redress exceeds EUR 1,000,000 per year.[33] According to the Energy Ombudsman, despite over 100 relevant recommendations being sent to energy companies, they have not been followed by the companies.

The chances of a successful collective settlement were low for at least two reasons. First, the competent Minister for Consumer Affairs had previously signed an agreement with the energy providers that authorised charging customers with the full year fee even if the customer terminated the contract before the end of the year. Secondly, there is uncertainty whether the Energy Ombudsman itself had a legal standing to initiate class action proceedings as under Belgian law such a class action could be brought only by the Consumer Ombudsman Service and not directly by its members.

In 2019, the court ordered a judgment regarding the procedural matters. The decision was appealed and the claim was declared inadmissible. The Court of Appeals held that the Consumer Ombudsman Service had failed to demonstrate any intent to negotiate, which the court considered a prerequisite for admissibility. Further, it found that the case in practice was run by the Energy Ombudsman, which was not entitled to bring class actions.[34]

2.1.2.4 *The Ryanair* case

One of the most interesting class actions was brought by Testachats against Ryanair in July 2019.[35] As a result of the four days of strikes that took place in summer 2018, many flights to and from Belgium were delayed or cancelled.[36] According to Testachats, passengers were not sufficiently informed

32 Belgian Consumer Ombudsman Services: http://www.neon-ombudsman.org/2018/09/26/the-belgian-energy-ombudsman-initiates-a-collective-redress-action-against-hidden-termination-fees/ (access 10.10.2023).

33 Belgian Consumer Ombudsman Services: http://www.neon-ombudsman.org/wp-content/uploads/2018/09/Press_release_Group-litigation_fixed-fees_20180925.pdf (access 10.10.2023).

34 Court of Appeal of Brussels, judgement of 14.04.2021, case file no. 2019/AR/1763 (unpublished).

35 Testachats: https://www.test-achats.be/actions-collectives/ryanair (access:10.10.2023).

36 A similar situation took place in the UK, where the Civil Aviation Authority started legal action against Ryanair after the company terminated the agreement with an alternative dispute resolution body: https://www.bbc.co.uk/news/business-46451702.

in advance about the potential for strike delays. Almost 170 flights were cancelled or delayed, which affected almost 40,000 passengers.

Under EU law, consumers may claim compensation in the amount of EUR 250 to EUR 600 for flight delays, depending on the flight distance.[37] However, Ryanair refused to compensate the customers saying that 'extraordinary circumstances' occurred and the strikes were outside of its power to be prevented.[38] Under Regulation 261/2004, an operating air carrier shall not be obliged to pay compensation if it can prove that the cancellation of the flight was caused by extraordinary circumstances that could not have been avoided even if all reasonable measures had been taken.[39]

The argument posed by Ryanair seems to be doubtful in light of the recent judgment of the European Court of Justice. In case C-195/17, the court ruled that the airlines must compensate their passengers for flight delays and cancellations even though the reason for this was a strike of their own staff.[40] The Court ruled that

> the spontaneous absence of a significant part of the flight crew staff ("wildcat strikes"), such as that at issue in the disputes in the main proceedings, which stems from the surprise announcement by an operating air carrier of a restructuring of the undertaking, following a call echoed not by the staff representatives of the company but spontaneously by the workers themselves who placed themselves on sick leave, is not covered by the concept of 'extraordinary circumstances' within the meaning of that provision.[41]

The class action against Ryanair was pending before the Brussels Commercial Court. The introductory hearing took place in September 2019. After the decision on the admissibility of the claim was issued in 2020, the court imposed an opt-in model. The case was settled in 2021 with Ryanair compensating passengers for the strikes.[42] All members of the group were entitled to a voucher

37 Regulation (EC) No. 261/2004 of the European Parliament and of the Council of 11 February 2004 establishing common rules on compensation and assistance to passengers in the event of denied boarding and of cancellation or long delay of flights, and repealing Regulation (EEC) No. 295/91, OJEU L 46/1, Art. 7 a)-c).

38 Brussels Times: https://www.brusselstimes.com/all-news/business/60496/test-achats-starts-class-action-suit-against-ryanair/ (access 10.10.2023).

39 Regulation (EC) No 261/2004, *op. cit*, Article 5 (3).

40 Judgment of the European Court of Justice dated 17 April 2018 in case C-195/17 *Krüsemann and Others* v. *TUIfly GmBH*, ECLI:EU:C:2018:258.

41 *Ibidem*, para. 48.

42 Euroconsumers: https://www.euroconsumers.org/major-win-for-ryanair-passengers-from-euroconsumers-member-ocu/ (access 10.10.2023).

up to EUR 600. In case the voucher is not used within the year, it could be exchanged for cash payment.[43]

2.1.2.5 *The Apple* case

The most recent class action was filed by the end of 2020 by Testachats against Apple.[44] The case concerns the allegedly unfair practice of Apple that caused integrated planned obsolescence of the Apple 6 iPhones. As a result of this practice, the phones deteriorated faster, which encouraged users to buy new products. The lawsuit asks for compensation in the amount of, on average, EUR 60 for each affected consumer. Testachats asked for an opt-out group participation. In October 2022, there was a hearing on the admissibility of the claim. The proceeding is still ongoing. Although there is nothing publicly available about this case, Testachats plans to plea admissibility in December 2024, and it contends that Apple continues to seek ways to expedite the process by incorporating formal elements and questions. No final decision on admissibility is expected before summer 2025.[45]

2.2 The Netherlands[46]

In contrast to many other EU Member States, the Netherlands has one of the most well-established, innovative and progressive systems of collective redress. It is innovative for at least three reasons: (i) it expressly allows for third-party funding[47], (ii) it is based on the more effective opt-out principle of group membership, and (iii) it benefits not only Dutch but also foreign consumers. It is progressive since it evolved from a system allowing for out-of-court settlements only to a system enabling collective actions for damages.[48]

The legislative framework for the Dutch system of collective redress is based on two regulations: (i) the 2005 Dutch Collective Settlement Act (*Wet Collectieve Afwikkeling Massaschade*, hereinafter referred to as WCAM) and (ii) the 2020 Act on the Resolution of Mass Claims in Collective Actions (*Wet Afwikkeling Massaschade in Collectieve Actie*, hereinafter referred to as WAMCA). WCAM has a been in use for nearly 20 years. While a still fairly new statute, WAMCA's usefulness in providing consumer redress is already

43 Testaankoop: https://www.test-aankoop.be/familie-prive/reizen/pers/akkoord-ta-ryanair (access 10.10.2023).

44 Testachats: https://www.test-achats.be/actions-collectives/apple-iphone (access 10.10.2023).

45 Euroconsumers: https://www.euroconsumers.org/apple-class-action-lawsuits/ (access 10.10.2023).

46 This section builds on the research findings drawing on the author's publication: Mucha (2021).

47 For details on third-party funding in the Netherlands, see: Kramer (2024: 778); Tillema (2022: 238); Augenhofer, Dori (2023: 204).

48 Tzankova, Kramer (2021: 97); Tillema (2022: 238).

being recognised.[49] The mechanisms provided in WCAM and WAMCA may be used in a wide range of matters, including (but not limited to) enforcement of consumer rights. Both procedures enable consumers to obtain compensation. Since collective redress in the Netherlands was already well-established, implementation of RAD resulted only in a few minor adaptations to the existing legislature landscape.[50] The following discussion will review the mechanisms under both WCAM and WAMCA and provide relevant examples of how said mechanisms operate in practice.

2.2.1 Collective settlements under the Dutch Collective Settlement Act

The introduction of WCAM in 2005 was considered a significant step towards a more efficient resolution of mass damage claims in the Dutch legal system.[51] The Act sets forth a unique mechanism providing that class actions are admissible only if a collective settlement is reached.[52] WCAM provides for a specific procedure in cases involving declarations that collective settlements of damage claims are binding.[53] The proceedings may be divided into four phases.

The first part of the proceedings under WCAM is entirely private and is not subject to court supervision. Instead, the parties to the dispute confer in an attempt to reach a settlement. On behalf of the claimant, it is reached by the Dutch foundation or association with full legal competence representing the interests of the members of the group. The legal standing of such entities is particularly important in the context of the commencement of the procedure recognising the settlement as binding before the court (second phase of the proceedings). On behalf of the defendant, the settlement is concluded by one or more parties who have engaged themselves under the settlement to pay compensation for the damage.

In the second phase of proceedings, the parties to the settlement jointly initiate the procedure recognising the collective settlement as binding. They submit a joint petition to the Amsterdam Court of Appeal (having exclusive competence to take cognisance in first instance of a request) in which they request the court to make the agreement binding for persons to whom the damage was caused. Dutch law specifies the admissibility criteria for such requests for recognition and the settlement itself.[54] The agreement on collec-

49 Klein, Rutten (2023: 11).
50 Weber (2024: 313).
51 Arons, van Boon (2010: 857); Tzankova, Hensler (2013: 94).
52 Kramer (2013: 74).
53 Krans (2014: 285).
54 Article 1018c of the Dutch Code of Civil Procedure.

tive settlement shall be attached as an appendix to the request. It must include: (i) a description of the event(s) to which the agreement relates, (ii) a description of the group(s) of people on whose behalf the agreement was concluded, specifying the nature and the seriousness of their loss, (iii) the accurate number of persons belonging to the group(s), (iv) the compensation that will be awarded to these persons, (v) the conditions that these persons must meet to qualify for the compensation, (vi) the procedure by which the compensation will be established and can be obtained, and (vii) the name and domicile of the persons to whom the written notification regarding the opt-out procedure must be submitted.[55]

The court shall reject the request if the agreement does not comply with the provisions specified. The court has influence on the merits of the collective settlement. Among others, it can reject the request of the parties under the following conditions: the amount of compensation is not reasonable, if it is insufficiently certain that the rights of the members of the group resulting from the agreements can be performed, or if the interests of persons on whose behalf the agreement was concluded cannot be adequately safeguarded. Before making a decision, the court may, with the approval of the parties, amend the agreement or offer the parties an opportunity to add further contractual provisions to the agreement to change its content.

The collective settlement procedure specified in WCAM follows an opt-out approach, meaning that the whole group is composed of individuals who claim to have been harmed by the same or similar infringement. Unless the members opt out from the group, they will receive the benefits from the judgment approving the settlement. Conversely, those members not opting out cannot seek compensation individually. WCAM provides a specific, detailed procedure for the members' participation in the group. In line with the opt-out approach, a copy of the decision to declare the collective settlement agreement binding is sent by post individually to all the persons known to be entitled to the compensation and to the foundations or associations that appeared at the proceedings. Additionally, after the decision has become irrevocable, a notice about the court decision is published in one or more newspapers, designated by the court. The notice includes a brief description of the agreement and the method by which the compensation can be obtained and, if the agreement provides so, the period within which the claim for compensation must be made, as well as the consequences of the declaration that the agreement is binding. Most importantly, the notice must include information about the period within which and the procedure by which persons entitled to the compensation can free themselves from the consequences of the declaration that the agreement is binding.

55 Article 7:907 par. 2 of the Dutch Civil Code.

In the third part of the proceedings a person entitled to the compensation who does not wish to be bound by the agreement must notify this in writing, within the period determined by the court (at least 3 months following the announcement of the court decision). The declaration that the agreement is binding has no consequences for any person who opted out within the specified time frame. Additionally, it does not bind any person entitled to compensation who was unaware of his damage at the time of the announcement but who has notified a person mentioned in the settlement agreement in writing after becoming aware of his damage that he does not want to be bound by the agreement.

In the fourth phase of the proceedings, compensation is to be paid to all members of the group who have not opted out.

2.2.2 Collective settlements under WCAM in practice—case studies

Although WCAM was introduced nearly 20 years ago, the mechanism of collective settlement has been used to conclude only nine settlements that were declared binding by the Amsterdam Court of Appeal. Initially, the introduction of WCAM in the Netherlands attempted to respond to the problem of mass harm. For the first time this law was used in the product liability case *DES*.[56] Before WCAM, it was impossible to claim compensation for injured persons collectively[57] and Dutch law lacked the possibility to force the injured persons into settling mass claims with some degree of finality.[58]

2.2.2.1 *The DES* case

The case concerned several thousand women who developed cervical and breast cancer as a result of the application of the DES hormone during pregnancy. The Dutch Supreme Court examined the issue of causation between physical injuries and the taking of medicines, including the DES hormone, by women and found that the pharmaceutical industry was liable for the injuries. Although the DES manufacturers wanted to reach a settlement, under Dutch law a settlement could only be made individually. As the total number of women potentially harmed by DES was estimated at more than 400,000, statutory legislation was needed to make the collective settlement binding. The victims were represented by the DES Centre, an organisation that was created in order to protect the interests of the DES daughters (daughters of women who took DES may develop a range of reproductive changes and fertility

56 Tillema (2016).
57 Hodges, Voet (2018: 125).
58 Arons, van Boon (2010: 865).

problems). The DES manufacturers established a EUR 35 million fund to pay compensation to the victims, provided that the settlement was final for all the Dutch victims. In order to manage the settlement, the Dutch Ministry of Justice sought a general solution that could also be applied in similar cases in the future. As a result of the DES case, WCAM was introduced. After the legislation was enacted in 2006, the Amsterdam Court of Appeal declared the settlement binding.[59]

2.2.2.2 *The Converium* case

Although WCAM was initially designed to respond to problems with the management of the product liability case, over the years it was used in cases involving financial products and securities.[60] One of the most well-known collective settlements under WCAM was the *Converium* case. It concerned Swiss reinsurance company Converium and Zurich Financial Securities (ZFS), which owned shares in Converium. The shares were listed on the Swiss Stock Exchange and on the New York Stock Exchange (as American depository shares). After ZFS had sold the shares through a public offering, the value of the shares plummeted since Converium increased its loss reserves. As a result, a number of class actions were brought by investors from various jurisdictions. In the United States, a class settlement was reached that was binding only for the US class members. Therefore, in 2012, investors from different jurisdictions (including the Netherlands, the UK and Switzerland) concluded a parallel settlement, which was brought to the Amsterdam Court of Appeal. Among other things, the court ruled that it had international jurisdiction to approve the settlement of the claims of non-US class members. Such a ruling was viewed as surprising since in the case there was no explicit link to the Netherlands. The claims were not brought under Dutch law, the shares were not traded on the Dutch stock exchange, the alleged wrongdoing took place outside the Netherlands, and none of the potentially liable parties and only a limited number of the potential claimants were domiciled in the Netherlands.[61] In its decision, the court held that the settlement of EUR 58 million was binding on all the class members. Moreover, the court ruled that the American lawyers involved in the settlement could receive a contingency fee in the amount of 20% of the settlement. In the international legal environment, the decision was widely discussed and Amsterdam was called a global hub for international class settlements involving non-US class members.[62]

59 van der Elst, Weterings (2021: 276).
60 Bosters (2017: 54); van Boon (2009: 178).
61 Knigge, Wijnberg (2020: electronic source).
62 Hodges, Voet (2018: 128); Clifford Chance (2012).

2.2.2.3 *The Ageas (Fortis)* case

Another settlement approved by the Amsterdam Court of Appeal was in the *Ageas (Fortis)* case in 2018. The value of the case amounted to EUR 1.3 billion, and so far, it is the largest settlement of this kind approved of in Europe. The case concerned Ageas, the legal successor of Fortis—a Belgian-Dutch bank insurance group that started its international expansion. The dispute arose in relation to the takeover of one of the Dutch banks by the consortium of three banks, including Fortis. To finance the transaction, Fortis increased the amount of capital and issued new shares to the existing shareholders at a lower price. The dispute arose from the alleged misleading statements of Fortis towards its shareholders. When the shares of Fortis went down, the company announced that it was more seriously exposed to the US subprime market and decided to limit the dividend to the shareholders.[63] After the fall of Lehman Brothers, Fortis customers started to withdraw their deposits and the share price dropped again to the extent that there was a serious risk that Fortis would declare bankruptcy. In order to prevent bankruptcy, the Dutch and Belgian governments proposed nationalisation of Fortis. As a result, many proceedings against Fortis were initiated by its shareholders in Belgium, the Netherlands and in the US.

In 2016, all the parties reached a settlement that required Ageas to pay EUR 12 billion in compensation to all of its shareholders who held shares in the specific time frame. In 2016, the settlement was submitted to the Amsterdam Court of Appeal that declined to approve the settlement. The Court found that it should not vary the amount of compensation for active and passive claimants (who filled the legal proceedings before and after the settlement was announced, respectively). It also criticised the amount of fees paid to the organisation representing the shareholders. As a consequence, the parties concluded a revised settlement agreement which, among others, included a EUR 100 million increase in the settlement.[64] In 2018, the court approved the revised settlement agreement, with a five-month time period for shareholders to opt out.[65] As of the date of this book, more than EUR 1 billion has been paid as compensation to the shareholders[66] who did not opt out and filed the claims for payment.

63 Declève (2017: 51).

64 Revised settlement agreement in English is accessible online at: https://www.forsettlement.com/pdf/Second_Amended_and_Restated_Settlement_Agreement_E.PDF?v=1.3.3 (access 20.11.2023).

65 Corporate Finance Lab: https://corporatefinancelab.org/2018/07/16/revised-e13-billion-settlement-in-the-fortis-case-approved-by-dutch-court/ (access 20.11.2023).

66 Updated information regarding the settlement and amount of payments are available online: https://www.forsettlement.com/ (access 20.11.2023).

2.2.3 Collective actions under the Dutch Act on the Resolution of Mass Claims in Collective Actions

Before 2020, the Netherlands had a system of collective redress under which the representative entities (Dutch foundations or associations) could seek only a declaratory or injunctive relief on behalf of the class claimants. Compensation could be awarded to the group only by means of collective settlement approved by the Amsterdam Court of Appeal under WCAM. Since 1 January 2020, collective redress was extended by the new legislation—WAMCA. It allows foundations and associations acting on behalf of class members to claim damages arising out of the harm suffered. To make a claim for damages admissible, the collective action must relate to the event that took place on or after 15 November 2016. The former system, enabling seeking declaratory or injunctive reliefs only, remains in force with respect to collective actions arising out of the events that took place before 15 November 2016 and/or to the actions initiated before 1 January 2020.

WAMCA provides for specific requirements relating to the legal standing of the foundations and associations that may bring a class action. The requirements include: having full legal capacity and representing the interests of group members by virtue of the articles of association.[67] The interests must also be sufficiently safeguarded, which is reflected by the obligation of the entity bringing a representative collective action (i) to have a supervisory board, (ii) to provide appropriate and effective mechanisms for the participation or representation in the decision-making of the members of the group, (iii) to have sufficient resources to bear the costs of instituting class action,[68] (iv) to have a generally accessible internet page that includes several points of information, and (v) to have sufficient experience and expertise with regard to instituting and conducting legal claims.

Unlike WCAM, WAMCA provides that the Dutch courts have jurisdiction over the class action only if a sufficient link with the Netherlands exists. The class action has a sufficiently close relationship with the Dutch legal order when (i) the majority of the group members have their habitual residence in the Netherlands or (ii) the defendant is domiciled in the Netherlands and additional circumstances indicate a sufficient relationship with the Dutch legal order or (iii) the event or events to which the legal claim relates has or have taken place in the Netherlands.[69] Class actions initiated under WAMCA shall be brought to one of the district courts in the Netherlands. The general rule is that the claim shall be brought to the court in the place of the defendant's domicile.

67 Article 305a of the Dutch Civil Code.
68 Kramer et al (2024:36).
69 Article 305a para. 3 of the Dutch Civil Code.

Additionally, the court also verifies whether the collective action is more efficient and effective that than filing an individual claim (i.e., it verifies whether the factual and legal questions are similar to all the group members, whether the number of the persons affected is sufficient, and—in relation to the claims for damages—whether the members of the class individually or jointly have a sufficiently large financial interest in the claim).

An interesting *novum* provided by WAMCA is a Dutch central register for collective actions.[70] The representative entity submitting the class action is obliged to make a note of this action in a register within two days of submitting the claim.[71] For the purpose of consolidating several proceedings, within three months after the entry of the class action to the register, a different foundation or association meeting the criteria specified in Article 305a of the Dutch Civil Code may also institute a collective action relating to the same event or events, invoking similar factual and legal issues. The class action must be brought to the same court as where the class action previously entered in the register was filed. In such case, the judge shall designate the representative entity that is most suitable from among the entities who have brought class action as the exclusive representative, taking into account the size of the group, the size of the financial interests represented by the group, other activities that it performs, and previous activities or collective actions brought by such representative entity.

Within six weeks following the expiration of the three-month deadline for the entry of class action into the public register, the defendant shall submit the statement of defence. WAMCA provides an opt-out model of membership in the class action for the members of the group who have a domicile or residence in the Netherlands. It means that the Dutch members of the group will be automatically bound by the judgment of the court unless they opt out within the time frame determined by the court. However, for non-Dutch members of the group, the opt-in membership model is stipulated, which means that to benefit from the collective action, the members have to agree to be represented in the collective claim within the time frame specified by the court. At the request of the party, the court may determine that the opt-out model is also applicable to non-Dutch members of the group.

70 See: The Dutch Central Register for Collective Actions, available online: https://www.rechtspraak.nl/Registers/centraal-register-voor-collectieve-vorderingen#6f1c15a9-f3e8-4b9b-ab79-4b3bb766c72f6bc1d2e4-e511-4e04-bf16-8ad720b8f8b319 (access 30.05.2024). See also: Reisner, van Duin (2024:5).

71 Article 1018c of the Dutch Code of Civil Procedure.

2.2.4 Collective actions under WAMCA in practice—case studies

Although WAMCA was introduced only a few years ago, there has already been a growing number of cases filed to show its effectiveness. According to the public register of class actions, there have been 79 class actions have been brought to the Dutch courts since January 2020.[72] Fifteen cases have already been adjudicated or settled. An exquisitely detailed analysis of the cases has already been conducted in the literature in the context of third-party funding.[73] In what follows, I will discuss some of the most interesting cases that can serve as examples of the functioning WAMCA in practice, with focus on and the scope of the group actions and the problem of admissibility of claims.

2.2.4.1 *The Volkswagen* case

One of the most thought-provoking class actions so far concerns the international Volkswagen emission scandal, known commonly in the media as 'Dieselgate.' In September 2015, a German carmaker was found to have misled the authorities and consumers by installing defeat devices in diesel cars, which enabled cheating of emissions tests. Volkswagen group admitted that about 11 million cars worldwide, including 8 million cars in Europe, were equipped with such defeat devices.[74] The car manufacturer reached settlements with large groups of car owners, including those from the US, Canada and Australia. In the United States, the largest settlement obtained a USD 10 billion settlement fund for 500,000 diesel car owners. Unlike in the US, in the EU the legislation regarding collective redress was still fragmented to the extent that Volkswagen benefited from the lack of coordinated litigation in Europe. As an illustrative example, as a result of the settlement in Germany 230,000 consumers received only EUR 830 million compensation, which was a fraction of what the VW company paid to American car owners.

The introduction of WAMCA in January 2020 opened the door for a class action against Volkswagen Group in the Netherlands.[75] The case was brought in March 2020 before the Amsterdam District Court by the Diesel Emission Justice Foundation (DEJF).[76] DEJF requested the court to be appointed as an exclusive representative of the Dutch buyers (opt-out membership) and non-Dutch buyers, residing or based in the EU Member States (opt-in membership). DEJF alleged that the Volkswagen Group intentionally and systemi-

72 *Ibidem*; see also Kramer (2024: 773).

73 Kramer et al. (2024: 82)

74 Hotten (2015: electronic source).

75 Celis (2020: electronic source).

76 See: Writ of summons is available on the website of the Dutch Central Register for Collective Actions: https://www.rechtspraak.nl/SiteCollectionDocuments/dagvaarding-collectieve-vordering-volkswagen-cs.pdf (access 10.10.2023).

cally manipulated 8.5 million European vehicles to pass emissions tests. DEJF claimed that the consumers suffered damages since they bought cars fitted with a defeat device that they would not have bought if they had known about it and its effects, or they had done so but under other conditions.[77] According to DEJF

> the residual value of the affected vehicles fell drastically as the Diesel Scandal became public. In addition, affected vehicles consumed more fuel, had higher maintenance costs and offered poorer driving performance. Lastly, DEJF claimed that the affected vehicles are in danger of becoming obsolete due to the introduction of environmental zones in inner cities and increasing nitrogen problems in general.[78]

In view of this, DEJF sought: (i) annulment, termination and cancelation of purchase agreements concluded between VW dealers and affected parties or lease(s) on the basis which the affected vehicles were made available to the affected buyers; (ii) the provision of the new vehicle that in terms of performance, driving style, appearance and value is similar to the affected vehicle; and (iii) damages.

In March 2022, the Amsterdam District Court ruled on its jurisdiction and lack of the applicability of WAMCA to this case.[79] The court found that it had jurisdiction over claims on behalf of Dutch car owners, but not other EU residents who bought their cars from a non-Dutch car dealer. As a result of the finding that WAMCA did not apply to the proceeding, DEJF could demand only a declaratory statement and not damages in the proceedings. DEJF appealed, and currently, the case is pending before the Amsterdam Court of Appeal. The decision on the applicability of WAMCA and international jurisdiction is expected in 2024.[80]

Over time, it became clear that Dieselgate was not limited to just one car manufacturer. Therefore, DEJF and other foundations brought more class actions before Dutch courts relating to similar Dieselgate emissions scandals. Before the Amsterdam District Court, there are cases pending against Daimler AG (producer of Mercedes Benz vehicles, its Dutch importers and individual

77 *Ibidem*; see also the description of the case provided by the DEJF in English, available online: https://ps-image-bucket.s3.amazonaws.com/emissionsjustice/wp-content/uploads/2020/03/20200313-Dagvaarding-VW-et-al-EN-Summary2712.pdf para. 19 (access 10.10.2023).

78 *Op. cit.*

79 Amsterdam District Court (*Rechtbank Amsterdam*), judgment of 30.03.2022, ECLI:NL:RBAMS:2022:1541

80 Emission Justice: https://www.emissionsjustice.com/vehicle-vw/?navmake=volkswagen (access 10.04.2024).

dealers for the damages resulting from the use of manipulation software to falsify emission testing),[81] Fiat Chrysler and Renault.[82] The cases are pending.

2.2.4.2 *The Evolve Media* case

A different group of class actions that can be brought under WAMCA include cases for an ideological purpose that represent very little financial value. Such cases might be filed with more lenient criteria of admissibility. One such class action was brought in February 2020 by the Dutch foundation's Stop Online Shaming and EOKM Foundation against Evolve Media (owner of the website vagina.nl), which exploits nude images without the permission of the people in the picture.[83] Both foundations claim that when using hidden cameras, people do not know that they have been filmed. The foundations underline that such online shaming causes severe damage such as reputation damage, problems in the private sphere, social isolation, loss of work, fear and depression.[84] The aim of the class action was to stop privacy violations, to prevent such content from being offered online again, and to ensure that the wrongdoers cannot hide behind false names.

The proceedings were brought before the Amsterdam District Court, which found that the foundations were admissible to submit the class action. In March 2021, the court ordered the proceedings to follow the opt-out model for the Dutch and opt-in for non-Dutch residents. The deadline for opt-out or opt-in was set for April 2021. In February 2022, the court issued a declaratory judgment stating that by publishing images online, the defendant was acting unlawfully unless it satisfied that those persons consented to publication. The Court ruled that the defendant is obliged to compensate the damage to the persons depicted in the visual material and to remove the content from the website. The judgment is vital for any future follow-up litigations and class actions against the website for commercially exploiting sexual images. It states that it is not necessary to prove the unlawfulness of each image/video since the images are unlawful even if people are unknown.[85]

81 Writ of summons is available on the website of the Dutch Central Register for Collective Actions: https://www.rechtspraak.nl/SiteCollectionDocuments/dagvaarding-collectieve-vordering-Daimler-AG-c.pdf (access: 11.11.2023); see also information on the website of the DEJF Foundation: https://www.emissionsjustice.com/wp-content/uploads/2020/06/Daimler-press-release-EN-2020062350.pdf (access: 22.11.2023).

82 Amsterdam District Court (*Rechtbank Amsterdam*), judgment of 10.04.2024, ECLI:NL:RBAMS:2024:2019 judgment on admissibility of claim.

83 See: Writ of summons is available on the website of the Dutch Central Register for Collective Actions: https://www.rechtspraak.nl/SiteCollectionDocuments/dagvaarding-collectieve-vordering-vagina.nl.pdf (access: 22.11.2023).

84 Stop online shaming campaign: https://www.stoponlineshaming.org/.

85 Amsterdam District Court (*Rechtbank Amsterdam*), judgment of 16.02.2022, ECLI:NL:RBAMS:2022:557.

2.2.4.3 *The Oracle* case

Representative actions might be a tool for collective private enforcement of data protection. An example of such a case is the class action against the technology group Oracle under the Privacy Collective Foundation in August 2020.[86] According to the Privacy Collective Foundation, Oracle and Salesform.com violated the General Data Protection Regulation[87] (GDPR) by using cookies to collect data from Dutch people. The information was distributed amongst online advertisers without the user's consent.[88] The foundation claimed that such misuse of personal data violated the right to privacy and family life and their right to the protection of personal data, arising out of the EU Charter of Fundamental Rights, GDPR and the Dutch Telecommunication Act. The alleged breach of the law consisted of (i) the application of automated decision-making, (ii) processing personal data without legal basis, (iii) non-transparent processing, (iv) infringement of the principle of data minimalisation, and (v) the unlawful transmission of personal data to the US.[89] The Privacy Collective Foundation sought monetary damages in the amount of EUR 500 per victim per company (Oracle and Salesform). With an assumed class of 10 million people affected, the total value of the claim is believed to be EUR 10 billion in damages.

In December 2021, the Amsterdam District Court decided that the claim was not admissible since the Private Collective Foundation did not meet the representativeness requirement.[90] The Court questioned the mechanism according to which the group members were identified. To join the group, the members were supposed to click on the support button on the website. However, it was not clear what the support was for, as the data breach was not mentioned on the support button. The Private Collective Foundation was not able to substantiate how many victims actually joined the class action and what the size of the claim it represents. The organisation did not formally register the data of those who push the button ; it only had the IP addresses of the website's visitors. As a result, the court adjudicated that the organisation brought the claim without the support of the group—the Private Collective was not sufficiently represented—and therefore, the claim was inadmissible.

86 See: Summons available on the website of the Dutch Central Register for Collective Actions: https://www.rechtspraak.nl/SiteCollectionDocuments/RBAMS-dagvaarding-collectieve-vordering-Oracle-Nederland-BV-SFDC-Netherlands-BV-Oracle-Corporation-Oracle-America-Inc-Salesforce.pdf (access 10.10.2023).

87 Regulation (EU) 2016/679 of the European Parliament and of Council of 27.04.2016 on the protection of natural persons with regard to the processing of personal data and on the free movement of such data, and repealing Directive 95/46/EC (General Data Protection Regulation).

88 https://theprivacycollective.eu/en/.

89 Point 4.6.1–4.6.5 of the Summons, *op. cit*.

90 Amsterdam District Court (*Rechtbank Amsterdam*), judgment of 29.12.2021, ECLI:NL:RBAMS:2021:7647 (in appeal).

2.3 England and Wales[91]

Since the UK left the EU, the UK legal system obviously does not need to implement EU directives anymore, and RAD is no exception here. Nonetheless, this jurisdiction is still worth reviewing as collective redress instruments are fairly well-established in England and Wales. Under English law, there exists three main structures enabling collective redress, namely: the representative actions, the group litigation order (GLO) and the collective procedure for consumers in competition law.

The first mechanism—representative actions—enables individuals to bring an action on behalf of other parties without their consent, where the represented parties share the same interest.[92] The 'same interests' are narrowly defined by the courts, and therefore, representative actions are allowed only for claimants with near identical fact patterns and loss to be grouped together.[93] Since in practice, the use of these mechanisms is of little use and relevance, especially in terms of consumer claims,[94] it will not be examined in what follows.

In contrast, the second means—GLO—is still the principal procedure of consumer collective redress in England and Wales. More than 120 GLOs have been initiated thus far, which compared to EU Member States, constitutes a considerable amount of cases.

The third approach in the UK is the collective procedure for consumers in competition law. This mechanism is particularly innovative since it involves two concepts that are still novel in EU law, namely it allows for an opt-out mechanism and for third-party funding. Ironically, EU law does not involve the right to representative actions for breach of competition law. However, due to the fact that the representative actions were adopted recently for the first time in EU legal history, the scope of RAD will hopefully be extended in the future also in the area of competition law.

2.3.1 Case management under Group Litigation Order

GLO is a mechanism that provides for the case management of individual claims, which gave rise to 'common or related issues of fact or law,' known as GLO issues. To put it simply, GLO is a case management tool for consolidating claims.[95] It is ordered by a court at the request of the parties or its own initiative. Application for GLO may be made either by a claimant or a

91 This section builds on the research findings drawing on the author's publication: Mucha (2021).
92 See: Civil Procedure Rules 1998, Part 19.6.
93 Ventrures (2019: electronic source).
94 Hodges, Voet (2018: 50).
95 Howells (2024: 279); Law (2021:321).

defendant at any time before or after any relevant claims have been issued. In support of the application for GLO, the applicant shall provide a summary of the nature of the litigation, the number and nature of claims already issued, the number of parties likely to be involved, the GLO issues that are likely to arise in the litigation, and information whether there are any matters that distinguish smaller groups of claims into the broader group.

The English Civil Procedure Rules (CRP) provide for some obligatory and facultative elements of GLO. Firstly, pursuant to the provisions of Article 19.13 of the CRP it must: (i) contain directions about the establishment of a register on which the claims managed under the GLO will be entered (called 'the group register'), (ii) specify the GLO issues that will identify the claims to be managed as a group under the GLO, and (iii) determine the court that will manage the claims on the group register (the 'managing court'). Once the GLO is ordered, the managing court may give directions regarding varying the GLO issues, providing for one or more claims on the group register to proceed as test claims, appointing the solicitor to be a lead solicitor for the claimants or defendants, specifying the details to be included in a statement of case in order to show that the criteria for entry of the claim to the register have been met, and specifying a date after which no claim may be added to the register unless the court gives permission to do so and for entry of any particular claim that meets one or more of the GLO issues on the group register.

The proceedings follow the opt-in regime, which means that potential members of the group must actively join the group in order to benefit from the judgment. Once the GLO is ordered, a group register is created, which involves the names of the claimants who are the parties to the GLO. The register is open for a specific time frame during which potential claimants may join the procedure. Maintaining and updating the group register is a task of the lead solicitor, as approved by the court. A judgment in the GLO is binding on the parties to all other claims that are signed in the group register at the time the judgment is given unless the court orders otherwise. The court may grant directions as to the extent to which that judgment is binding on the parties to any claim that is subsequently entered on the group register. Any party who is adversely affected by the judgment that is binding on him may seek permission to appeal the GLO.

2.3.2 GLO in practice—the Dieselgate case study

Over the past 25 years there were more than 120 group litigation orders issued by the courts in England and Wales.[96] One in five orders related to consumer protection. Although compared to other European jurisdictions this number

96 List of all group litigation orders issued in England and Wales since 1999 is published online at: https://www.gov.uk/guidance/group-litigation-orders#history (access 15.01.2024).

seems to be significant, the outcomes of the GLOs are not known, and therefore, it is difficult to say unequivocally whether GLO is an effective instrument allowing for consumer law enforcement.[97]

The most prominent example of successful group action in England and Wales was the one brought against Volkswagen.[98] The investigation shows that defeat devices were installed by the car manufacturer in 1.2 million cars owned in the UK. To date, the case is considered the largest consumer group action to come before the English courts. In March 2018 the GLO was issued by the High Court in London.[99] The legal action was brought on behalf of British car owners in 2018 under the Consumer Protection from Unfair Trading Regulation over allegations that Volkswagen had software fitted to their vehicles that cheated the EU emissions tests. Under the GLO, two law firms were appointed as leading solicitors. Advertisements about the GLO were published in the national newspapers in May 2018.[100] The potential claimants who wished to be added to the group register of claims had until October 2018 to contact solicitors in order to join the group action. One of the leading solicitors—Leigh Day law firm—claimed a refund of at least 50% of the value of the car or finance repayments. To join the group, the vehicle must have been bought for personal, not business use, from an approved dealer of VW group directly and paid for on or after October 2014. In total, in the group register the claims were registered by circa 91,000 consumers from the UK.

In April 2020, the High Court in London ruled in favour of the consumers. The court found that the decision of the German Road Vehicle Authority (*Kraftfahrtbundesamt*, KBA), stating that the affected vehicles contained a defeat device, was binding on the English courts. The court also decided that the fact that the engines operated in different modes during the emissions tests means that they contained a defeat device under the EU emissions regulations.[101] Volkswagen appealed this ruling, but its appeal was rejected by the court. According to the leading plaintiff, in spite of such a decision, VW group continued to deny the claims in the UK and it did not want to enter into settlement negotiations. According to VW, it did not owe compensation to consumers since they have not suffered any loss.

97 Hodges, Voet (2018: 53).

98 The facts of the case were the same as the one discussed above in relation to the consumer collective redress in the Netherlands.

99 https://www.gov.uk/government/publications/group-litigation-orders/list-of-group-litigation-orders#VW-NOx-emissions-group-litigation (access 11.11.2023).

100 The advertisement of the group action published in the newspaper: https://www.leighday.co.uk/getmedia/a9ff8ca0-9c1a-42c5-b97e-409ef9e7f0e4/The-VW-NOx-Emissions-Group-Litigation-ad2.aspx (access 11.11.2023).

101 Judgment of the Mr Justice Waksman as of 6.4.2020, available online: https://www.judiciary.uk/wp-content/uploads/2020/04/VWJudgment-002.pdf (access 20.11.2023).

The case was scheduled for a trial in early 2023. However, by the end of 2022, it was settled out of court. VW did not admit its liability, but it stated that the legal costs of the trial in England made the settlement more economically beneficial. The terms and conditions of the settlement were confidential, but it was publicly announced that the costs amounted to GBP 193 million plus. Each of the 91,000 group members received GBP 2,120 compensation. Additionally, VW paid a separate contribution for claimants' legal costs and other fees.

The massive VW settlement gave rise to other similar claims against other vehicle manufacturers, such as Mercedes, BMW, Fiat Chrysler, etc., accused of misconduct in relation to diesel emission fraud. Car owners hoped that a first-of-this-kind settlement with VW will set a precedent for future cases. Over 2,000,000 people signed up for the My Diesel Claim initiated by the Pogust Goodhead law firm in London.[102] The participants were able to join their claims as there is no risk of costs in a losing case—there is no fee and the company covers all legal costs. The law firm informs that car drivers, depending on a number of factors, may claim GBP 10,000 compensation. In case of a win, it caps the fees at the maximum of 50% inclusive tax. The company requested more than ten GLOs against different car manufacturers and so far there is no information about any further settlements.

2.3.4 Collective procedure for consumers in competition law

Another mechanism allowing for collective redress in England and Wales relates to claims for the breach of competition law. The proceeding is brought by the class representative before the Competition Appeal Tribunal (CAT), which decides whether to issue a so-called Competition Proceedings Order (CPO). Rule 79 of CAT[103] states that claims might be certified if (i) they are brought on identifiable class members, (ii) they raise the common issues, and (iii) are suitable to be brought in collective proceedings. Proceedings may follow an opt-in or opt-out approach, and the suitable model is to be determined by CAT *ad casum*. It can take into account all matters it thinks fit, including the strength of the claims and whether it is practicable for the proceedings to be brought as opt-in collective proceedings, having regard to all the circumstances, including the estimated amount of damages that individual class members may recover. After a CPO has been made, the class representative shall establish a register on which it shall record the names of those class members who, in accordance with Rule 82 of CAT, opt in to or opt out of the action.

102 https://mydieselclaim.com/ (access 10.05.2024).
103 Competition Appeal Tribunal Rules 2015 no. 1648.

Currently, there are 48 collective proceedings pending before CAT,[104] with the most significant case in UK legal history—*Merricks v. Mastercard*.[105] This sprawling claim was brought by the class representative—a former ombudsman of the Financial Ombudsman Service, Mr Merricks—on behalf of 45.5 million consumers. The size of the group was massive as the case follows an opt-out approach. The group consisted of all individuals who between 1992 and 2008, when aged 16 and above and resident in the UK, purchased goods or services from businesses selling in the UK that accepted Mastercard. The class representative estimated the damages in an amount of about GBP 10 billion. The collective proceeding was a follow-on action for damages arising out of the EU Commission decision on the infringement of the EU competition law,[106] namely Art. 101 of the Treaty on the Functioning of the EU. In 2014, the Court of Justice of the European Union upheld the Commission's decision stating that the fees for cross-border transactions charged by Mastercard were too high.[107]

The collective claim pending before CAT in *Merricks v. Mastercard* is based on the allegation that consumers in the UK paid too much for goods and services because of inflated interchange fees imposed by Mastercard on businesses that accepted credit and debit cards. The class representative claimed that fees for cross-border transactions were causative of the domestic interchange fees in the UK. Further, the domestic interchange fees were passed by acquiring banks in the charges to the business processing card transactions and finally, the fees were passed in prices charged to the customers in the UK. After a series of appeals and the decision of the Supreme Court, the Competition Proceedings Order was ordered by CAT in 2022, and the case was admissible. However, in a decision of February 2024, CAT rejected the allegations of the class representative that cross-border transaction fees had any significant causative influence on the level of interchange fees that applied to UK domestic transactions. The case is still pending; a trial on liability is scheduled for the second part of 2024.

2.4 Conclusion

Collective redress systems in Belgium, the Netherlands and England and Wales are not free from imperfections. Still, the analysis of the legislative framework for collective redress and its use in practice in the three above-mentioned jurisdictions allows me to draw some conclusions on the best

104 https://www.catribunal.org.uk/cases (access 10.05.2024).

105 *Walter Hugh Merricks* CBE v *Mastercard Incorporated and Others*, case no. 1266/7/7/16.

106 European Commission, decision no. COMP/34.579 and COMP/36.518.

107 Judgment of the CJEU of 11.09.2014, case C-382/12 P *Mastercard v. Commission*, ECLI:EU:C:2014:2201.

practices which, in my opinion, are worth implementing in other Member States.

Starting with Belgium, the discussion shows that the major entity involved on behalf of consumers is Testachats, which initiated nine out of ten proceedings. At present it is considered as the only entity capable of bringing representative action in practice, mostly because of its financial capabilities and expertise. Testachats is criticised as having the monopoly for collective redress in Belgium, however there is no other consumer organisation with comparative capabilities. Considering that the Belgian legislation on consumer collective redress was introduced ten years ago, the number of cases (approximately two per year) is not significant. However, it should be taken into account that the number of consumers involved in each of these cases was considerable, so—all in all—the actions for collective redress had an impact on the hundreds of thousands of consumers. This was possible, among others, thanks to the possibility of the court choosing between the opt-in or opt-out mechanism. The use of the opt-out mechanism meant a large number of affected consumers could be included. This freedom of the court to decide between an opt-in and opt-out model is a very interesting legal solution that is worth considering in other Member States.

Currently, the flexibility between the opt-in and opt-out model in Belgium is noticeable only during the negotiation phase of proceedings, when it is up to the parties to decide which model to follow. I think, however, that adopting this solution might be too far-reaching in some other jurisdictions, especially where there is no settlement culture. Poland would probably be one of such jurisdictions in which traders would not agree to an opt-out model and this flexibility would only delay the course of proceedings. Therefore, I believe that it is worth leaving the decision on group formation to the discretion of the court.

Additionally, it was noted that involving a huge number of consumers would not be possible without the activity of strong consumer organisations. Therefore, it is crucial to create such entities in other Member States that would not only be aware of consumer problems but, at the same time, would be capable of bringing collective actions in practice. Taking Poland as an example, it needs to be stated at this point that there is no such consumer organisation that could be comparable in terms of financial capacity and human resources to Testachats in Belgium.[108]

When compared to other Member States, the Dutch legal system is regarded as having the most advanced collective redress framework in the EU. What accounts for the Dutch success? Firstly, it allows the opt-out model of group formation for Dutch group members, which influences the size of the group represented. Further, the Dutch collective redress system is open

108 This problem is discussed in Chapter 3 of this book.

for many representative entities entitled to start class actions, mainly because it allows the *ad hoc* organisations to be created for the purpose of specific class action in domestic proceedings. Therefore, unlike in Belgium, where in practice the monopoly for class actions has Testachats, representative actions in the Netherlands are brought by many different representative entities. The plurality of entities operating in practice is possible thanks to commercial third-party funding, which is explicitly allowed in the Netherlands. Under WAMCA there is no cap on fees for the third-party funders and the amount of the benefit for the litigation funders depends on the amount of compensation awarded to consumers.[109] In one of the recent class actions (*Vatenfall*) the Dutch court allowed a 25% cap from the final compensation for the third-party funder.[110] The liberal attitude of the Dutch judges towards commercial litigation funding makes the Netherlands an interesting market for third-party funders, and it is expected that this interest will grow in the next few years.

Thanks to the existence of the group register, the Dutch system seems to be very transparent and accessible for consumers, especially taking into account that under WAMCA all the writs of summons are published online. It would be very beneficial to draw on Dutch experience and amend the Polish group register in a way that will enable potential consumers to become acquainted with the statement of the claim. Although the register of group proceedings exists under Polish law,[111] it includes only some basic information about the proceedings itself, which is not sufficient to decide whether to join the group. Additionally, it would be highly beneficial for other Member States to embrace the option of collective settlement without needing to initiate litigation.

Besides the Netherlands, the UK seems to be a favourable jurisdiction to bring class actions in Europe.[112] The English GLO system, although based on the opt-in approach, seems to be similar to the American class action system in the way that various law firms are competing in order to represent groups of consumers, requesting at the same time quite high success fees (including even 50% of the compensation awarded).[113] However, it is noted that in practice, it is difficult to fulfil the requirements set for the GLO, and therefore the total number of GLOs, amounting to five per year, is not significant. From this perspective, the GLO procedure might be perceived as not an effective way of seeking consumer redress. However, it shall also be noted that once the GLO is issued, the case involves mostly large groups of members and therefore, in case of judgments issued in favour of consumers, the GLO may affect the

109 Reyner, van Duin (2024: 4).

110 Kramer (2024: 779).

111 Polish register of group proceedings is available online: https://www.gov.pl/web/sprawiedliwosc/wykaz-postepowan-grupowych (access 12.11.2023).

112 Howells (2024: 287);

113 For controversies on recoverability of lawyers' success fees in England and Wales see: Stadler (2022: 155)

situation of a wide range of harmed persons. Due to the fact that the outcomes of the GLO's proceedings are not known, it is impossible to assess whether the consumers can really benefit from the judgments.

Following the English experience, an interesting option to be considered in EU Member States is the possibility of requesting group proceedings by the defendant at any time before or after any relevant claims have been issued. For reasons of procedural economy, not only claimants, but also defendants might be interested in participation in one group proceeding instead of being bundled by many individual litigations.

Finally, it would be vital to follow the English approach and to allow the representative actions in competition law in the EU in the future. Currently, under RAD, this area is excluded, since competition law is not mentioned in Annex I, which specifies the scope of RAD.[114] The English experience shows that class action cases regarding the infringement of competition law are massive cases that include millions of people. In practice, this kind of case shall be covered by representative actions that are tailored to solve the problem of mass harm. The mere possibility of a class action in antitrust cases, along with the potential for significant compensation, may deter traders from violating consumer rights, thereby enhancing consumer protection in the EU.

References

Amaro R, Azar-Baud M J, Corneloup S, Fauvarque-Cosson B, Jault-Seseke F (2018). *Collective redress in the Member States of the European Union.* Study commissioned by the European Parliament.

Arons T, van Boon W H (2010) Beyond tulips and cheese: Exporting mass securities claim settlements from the Netherlands, *European Business Law Review*, Vol. 21(6), pp. 857–883.

Augenhofer S, Dori A (2023) The proposed regulation of third party litigation funding – much ado about nothing?, *Zeitschrift für das Privatrecht der Europäischen Union*, Vol. 5, pp. 198–209.

Azar-Baud M J et al (2024) *Compare-and-contrast analysis of collective redress mechanisms across ten jurisdictions in the European Union*, Digital Freedom Fund, electronic source: https://digitalfreedomfund.org/digirise/collective-redress-database/

Biard A (2024) Transposition of directive (EU) 2020/1828 in France: A second wind for collective action? *Revue européenne de droit de la consommation (R.E.D.C.)*, Vol. 2, pp. 231–254.

van Boon WH (2009) Collective settlement of mass claims in the Netherlands, In: Casper M et al (eds), *Auf dem Weg zu einer europäischen Sammelklage?* Sellier, pp. 171–192.

Bosters T (2017) *Collective redress and private international law in the EU*, Springer.

114 Vlahek (2024: 53); Hornkohl (2024: 311).

Boularbah H, van den Bossche M (2018) Belgium, In: Swallow R (ed), *Class action law review*, Law Business Research Ltd, pp. 14-27.

Bugatti L (2024) The Directive (EU) 2020/1828 and the consumer representative actions in Italy: A step back or forward? *Revue européenne de droit de la consommation (R.E.D.C.),* Vol. 2, pp. 289–312.

Celis M (2020) *The Volkswagen (VW) emissions scandal- the saga continues: now it's the turn of the Netherlands*, electronic source: https://conflictoflaws.net/2020/the-volkswagen-vw-emissions-scandal-the-saga-continues-now-its-the-turn-of-the-netherlands-france-and-belgium/.

Clifford Chance (2012) *The converium decision: Promoting the Netherlands as a centre for class settlements*, electronic source: https://www.cliffordchance.com/content/dam/cliffordchance/briefings/2012/02/the-converium-decision-promoting-the-netherlands-as-a-centre-for-class-settlements.pdf.

CMS (2023) *2023 European class actions report*, electronic source: https://cms.law/en/media/international/files/publications/publications/european-class-action-report-2023?v=2.

Declève Q (2017) Fortis's settlement: A comparative case study of securities class action mechanisms in Europe and the United States, *Business Law International*, Vol. 18(1), pp. 51–72.

van der Elst C, Weterings W (2021) The Dutch mechanisms for collective redress: Solid, and excellent within the reach, In: Fitzpatrick B, Randal T (eds), *The Cambridge handbook of class actions. An international survey*, Cambridge University Press, pp. 272–302.

Hodges C, Voet, S (2018) *Delivering collective redress: New technologies*, Hart Publishing.

Hornkohl L (2024) Collective actions for competition law violations and DMA infringements following the transposition of the representative actions directive (Germany), *Journal of European Competition Law and Practice*, Vol. 15 (5), pp. 311–317.

Hotten R (2015) Volkswagen: The scandal explained, *BBC*, electronic source: https://www.bbc.com/news/business-34324772.

Howells G (2024) Class actions in the UK and Ireland. A tale of two common laws diverging post-Brexit, *Revue européenne de droit de la consommation (R.E.D.C.),* Vol. 2, pp. 277–288.

Inga L J (2024) *Assessing collective private parties' litigation in the economy of data. Country report: Belgium (applied project)*, electronic source: https://act.uva.nl/research/research-projects/applied/country-reports.html.

Klein J, Rutten K (2023) *Three years of WAMCA- a second quantitative analysis*, electronic source: https://www.deminor.com/en/wamca/.

Knigge A, Wijnberg I (2020) *Class/collective actions in the Netherlands: Ōverview*, electronic source: https://www.houthoff.com/-/media/houthoff/publications/aknigge/thomson-reuters_class_collective-actions-in-the-netherlands_overview.pdf.

Kramer X (2013) Enforcing mass settlements in the European judicial area: EU policy and the strange case of Dutch collective settlements (WCAM), In: Stadler A, Hodges C (eds), *Resolving mass disputes: ADR and settlement of mass claims*, Edward Elgar, pp. 63–90.

Kramer X (2024) The quest for funding under the utch WAMCA: Third party funding and the viability of a procedural fund, *Emory International Law Review*, Vol. 38(4), pp. 765–784.

Kramer X et al (2024) *Financing collective redress actions in the Netherlands: Towards a litigation fund?* Eleven.

Kramer X, Tillema I (2020) The funding of collective redress by entrepreneurial parties: The EU and Dutch context, *Revista Ítalo-Española de Derecho Procesal*, Vol. 2020(2), pp. 165–181.

Krans B (2014) The Dutch act on collective settlement of mass damages, *Pacific McGeorge Global Business & Development Law Journal*, Vol. 27(2), pp. 281–301.

Law S (2021) Public and private enforcement of consumer law in England and Wales, In: Law S, Richard V (eds), *Public and private enforcement of consumer law-Insights for Luxembourg*, Nomos, pp. 291–344.

Mucha J (2019) Consumer protection in practice- transnational comparative account of collective redress mechanisms- part one: The Belgian approach, *Humanities and Social Sciences*, Vol. 26(4), pp. 93–103.

Mucha J (2021) Consumer protection in practice- transnational comparative account of collective redress mechanisms- part two: The Dutch and the English approaches, *Humanities and Social Sciences Quarterly*, Vol. 28 (1), pp. 73–87.

Nowak J T (2021) Public and private enforcement of consumer law in Belgium, In: Law S, Richard V (eds), *Public and private enforcement of consumer law- insights for Luxembourg*, Nomos, pp. 113–246.

Reisner M, van Duin A (2024) *Assessing collective private parties' litigation in the economy of data. Country report: The Netherlands* (applied project), electronic source: https://act.uva.nl/research/research-projects/applied/country-reports.html

Riefa C, Saintier S (2021) In search of (access to) justice for vulnerable consumers, In: Riefa C, Saintier S (eds), *Vulnerable consumers and the law. Consumer protection and access to justice*, Routledge, pp. 1–16.

Rott P (2024) The new German representative actions- a mixed bag, *Revue européenne de droit de la consommation (R.E.D.C.),* Vol. 2, pp. 255–276.

Stadler A (2022) Third-party funding in collective redress, In Kramer X et al (eds), *Delivering justice: A holistic and multidisciplinary approach liber amicorum in honour of Christopher Hodges*, Hart Publishing, pp. 151–160.

Steennot R (2024) The transposition of the representative actions directive in Belgium, *Revue européenne de droit de la consommation (R.E.D.C.),* Vol. 2, pp. 185–209.

Stein K (2024) Representative actions for protection of the collective interests of consumers: Estonian experiences, *Revue européenne de droit de la consommation (R.E.D.C.),* Vol. 2, pp. 211–230.

Tillema I (2016) Entrepreneurial motives in Dutch collective redress: Adding fuel to a "compensation culture"? In: Van Boon WH (ed), *Litigation, costs, funding and behavior: Implications for the law*, Routledge, pp. 222–243.

Tillema I (2022) Dutch collective actions and the rise of entrepreneurial actors: Navigating between access to justice and a claim culture, In Kramer X et al (eds), *Frontiers in civil justice*, Privatisation, Monetisation and Digitisation, pp. 238–258.

Tzankowa I, Hensler D (2013) Collective settlements in the Netherlands: Some empirical observations, In: Stadler A, Hodges C (eds), *Resolving mass disputes: ADR and settlement of mass claims*, Edward Elgar, pp. 91–105.

Tzankova I, Kramer X (2021), From injunctions and settlement to action: Collective redress and funding in the Netherlands In: Uzelac A, Voet S (eds.), *Class actions in Europe: Holy grail of a wrong trail?* Springer, pp. 97–130.

Ventrures A (2019) *To GLO or not to GLO- a funder's perspective*, Lexology, electronic source: https://www.lexology.com/library/detail.aspx?g=1c9a6bc7-6189-462a-a89c-56c5b146dc96.

Vlahek A (2024) The great saga of collective redress in EU competition law: all cry and no wool?, *World Competition*, Vol 74(1), pp. 53–72.

Voet S (2021) Class action in Belgium: Evaluation and the way forward, In: Uzelac A, Voet S (eds), *Class actions in Europe. Holy grail of a wrong trail?* Springer, pp. 131–163.

Voet S, Dethier S (2024) *Bridging the EU consumer enforcement pathways in mass harm situations*, BEUC.

Weber F (2024) Implementation in the Netherlands- the advanced pre-directive enforcement landscape, some data and lessons learnt, and minor changes brought about by the directive, *Revue européenne de droit de la consommation (R.E.D.C.),* Vol. 2, pp. 313–330.

3 Pursuing consumer collective claims in group proceedings in Poland

The landscape of consumer law enforcement in Poland is currently very widespread. Prior the implementation of the Representative Actions Directive (RAD), a clear distinction existed between private and public enforcement of consumer collective redress. Both paths of enforcement operated simultaneously, however, there was a very well-defined allocation of roles. Public enforcement of collective consumer interests was carried out through administrative proceedings, conducted by the Polish President of the Office of Competition and Consumer Protection (in Polish: *Prezes Urzędu Ochrony Konkurencji i Konsumentów*, hereinafter referred to as the 'President of UOKiK')—an administration authority responsible for implementing consumer protection policy. As a central government authority, it acts in the public interest and institutes proceedings concerning practices involving infringement of collective consumer rights and in cases concerning the classification of clauses in standard agreements as abusive.[1] Thereby, actions for injunctions stipulated under Directive 2009/22/EC were at the discretion of the President of UOKiK. This authority was the only entity recognised as a qualified entity entitled to start the injunction proceedings and, at the same time, it issued decisions on the injunction.[2] On the private path of law enforcement, consumers seek redress in civil proceedings before courts—either in individual or group proceedings (a Polish style of collective redress). The latter is discussed in this chapter.

After RAD was implemented in Poland, the strict division of consumer law enforcement between private and public sectors became blurred. In addition to the existing private and public split, the mechanism of representative actions has been integrated into the current framework. This mechanism primarily falls under private enforcement, as the representative entities in Poland pursue claims through group proceedings in court. The administrative authority—the President of UOKiK—retains the competence to initiate injunctive

1 Act of 16 February 2007 on Competition and Consumer Protection, (Journal of Laws of 2007, No. 50, item 331 with further amendments), hereinafter referred to as "the ACCP".
2 Mucha (2021: 35).

DOI: 10.4324/9781003520849-4

proceedings and issue decisions on injunctions, while also requiring important competencies in representative proceedings. Currently, the President of UOKiK maintains the register for representative entities and oversees compliance with the requirements specified for these entities under RAD. Actions for injunctions can now be initiated both by the President of UOKiK in administrative proceedings and by representative entities in court.

This chapter examines the complex landscape of consumer collective redress in Poland. It begins by presenting the legislative framework outlined in the Act of 17 December 2009 on Pursuing Claims in Group Proceedings (hereinafter referred to as the 'Act on Group Proceedings'),[3]to provide a backgroud for further discussion on data and analysis of relevant group proceedings. In this part of the study I critically analyse the statistical data published by the Ministry of Justice and the information included in the register of group proceedings. Next, this data is confronted with the findings of an evidence-based examination of cases, that has been conducted at the District Court in Warsaw (in Polish: *Sąd Okręgowy w Warszawie*). The findings are complemented by the outcomes of the interviews with different institutions and stakeholders involved in group proceedings- municipal/regional consumer ombudsmen (in Polish: *miejscy/powiatowi rzecznicy konsumentów*), Financial Ombudsman (in Polish: *Rzecznik Finansowy*), Polish Commissioner for Human RIghts (in Polish: *Rzecznik Praw Obywatelskich*), President of UOKiK and leading Polish attorneys representing the parties in group proceedings. Thereby, the chapter analyses how group proceedings function in practice. Finally, it examines the recent legislative changes introduced by the implementation of RAD in Poland and discusses some most important and, at the same time, controversial solutions, such as: liberalisation of admissibility requirements, principles of recognition of representative entities, costs of group proceedings, dual role of the President of UOKiK in the process of consumer law enforcement and the possibility of third-party funding. The chapter addresses whether and how the new law will alter the landscape of group proceedings in Poland and impact consumers' ability to enforce their rights collectively.

3.1 Legislative framework for collective redress in Poland

Compared to other Member States, Poland has quite a long tradition of collective redress. Since 2009, individuals have been able to seek redress measures in group proceedings before national courts (private path of enforcement). The collective redress mechanism was introduced by the Act on Group

3 Act of 17 December 2009 on Pursuing Claims in Group Proceedings, (Journal of Laws 2010, No. 7 item 44 with further amendments).

Proceedings, and according to the latest data, 319 group actions were submitted to Polish courts from 2010 to 2021 in this mode in civil cass.[4]

Under Article 3 of the Act on Group Proceedings, the higher disctrict courts (in Polish: *sądy okręgowe*) are competent for adjudicating cases in group proceedings. Their competence in this field is irrespective of the value of the individual claims or the aggregated value of the collective claims. The cases are adjudicated by the court composed by three judges. The judgment of the disctrict court is subject to appeal to court of appeal (in Polish: *sąd apelacyjny*) and further to the Supreme Court (in Polish: *Sąd Najwyższy*). Currently, there are 47 higher disctrict courts in Poland competent for adjudicating cases in group proceedings in the first instance and 11 courts of appeal.[5] The competence of the courts mentioned above remains relevant for consumer representative actions, within the meaning of RAD.

The course of Polish group proceedings has been extensively discussed in Polish literature, and there is no need to repeat those discussions here.[6] Although the implementation of RAD to Polish law brought some important changes to national legislation (that are discussed in the section 3.5. of this chapter), these amendments did not influence the general concept or course of group proceedings, which still comprise of a sequence of several stages. For purpose of clarity of further discussion on how group actions operate in practice, it is essential to outline some foundations that underpin the concept of group actions.

The scope of application of the Act on Group Proceedings is not limited to consumer claims only. In line with Article 1 section 2 of this act, collective actions can be brought in product liability claims, tort liability claims, claims for liability for non-performance or improper performance of a contract, and unjustified enrichement claims, as well as i all other matters that refer to consumer claims. The act excludes claims for the protection of personal interests from its scope, except for personal injury claims. Implementation of RAD extended the scope by adding consumer representative actions, that are actions for an injunction and actions for redress measures, to the existing scheme.

The Act on Group Proceedings establishes a four-stage course of proceedings that is specific to collective redress only. It consists of (i) certification,

4 Ministry of Justice, Opracowania wieloletnie: isws.ms.gov.pl/pl/baza-statystyczna/opracowania-wieloletnie/ (access 6.11.2023).

5 Regulation of the Polish Ministry of Justice as of 28.12.2018 on establishing seats and jurisdictions of the court of appeal, district courts and regional courts and the scope of adjudication (Journal of Laws 2021, Item 1269 with further amendments).

6 In Polish: Rejdak (2019: 33), Sieradzka (2018: 75), Asłanowicz (2018: electronic source), Laskowska-Hulisz(2022: 232); in English see: Tulibacka (2018: 138); Trzaska (2019: 155), Studzińska (2016: 162);Nekrosius and Flaga-Gieruszyńska (2021: 241).

(ii) group formation, (iii) proceedings regarding the substance of the case, and (iv) enforcement.

The proceedings begin with a lawsuit brought by a group representative. Collective action might be brought either by a member of this group, a regional (municipal) consumer ombudsman, or a Financial Ombudsman, with the latter acting within the scope of its prerogatives (Article 4).[7] A group representative acts on behalf of the group, it is a party to the proceedings. Except from Financial Ombudsman, it must be represented by a legal attorney. Apart from above mentioned entities entitled to start collective action, by the way of transposition of RAD, also so called 'qualified entities' (in Polish: *podmioty upoważnione*) are entitled to bring consumer representative actions. To be recognised as such, these qualified entites must fulfill specific criteria mentioned by the new law and apply to be registered by the President of UOKiK. Initiating proceedings by the municipal consumer ombudsman, Financial Ombudsman or qualified entity is particularily beneficial for group members, since these entites are not required to pay courrt fees, which are set as 2% of the value of the claim.

In the decision to certify the class action (decision on the admissibility of group proceedings) the court confirms that all requirements set for group proceedings are fulfiled. For a group action to be admissable, the collective action must be brought in the name of at least 10 people with claims of the same kind and with the same or a similar factual basis. In quite revolutionary way, implementation of RAD in Poland provided an exception to this rule. It states that in case of consumer represntative action, brought by qualified entities, claims might be based also on the same or a similar legal basis. Additionally, according to the general rule, in cases concerrning monetary claims, group proceedings are admissable only if the amount claimed by each group member has been made equal with the others (so called 'commonality requirement' included in Article 2 of the Act on Group Proceedings).The commonality requirement is excluded for all consumer collective claims (including consumer representative actions), which shall facilitate the greater admissibility of collective claims for the benefit of consumers. Alternatively, in cases concerning monetary claims, the claim may be limited to declaratory relief only. This situation occurs when the circumstances related to particular members are so diverse that it is impossible to fulfill commonality requirement. When declaratory relief is awarded, each group member may start separate follow-up proceedings and pursue claims individually.

Decision on admissibility also contains information about the action, the group representative, arrangements concerning the remuneration of lawyers

7 In reference to the classification of major forms of collective redress mentioned in the first chapter of this book it shall be noted that Polish group proceedings can either have a form of group action or representative action.

and the names of class members who have joined so far. It can be (and in practice, almost always is) appealable. In the case of negative verification of fulfilment of the requirements specified for group proceedings, the court rejects the action. In case of positive verification of the above-mentioned criteria in the final decision of the court, the admissibility of the claim is not verified at the later stages of the proceedings. The final decision on certification ends the first phase of the proceedings.

The second stage, known as group formation, follows an opt-in approach. It involves notifying all potential group members about the group action in the manner most appropriate for each case. In practice, for this purpose, the court issues an order to publish information regarding the group proceedings in the national or regional press. The court may also determine that no further notification is necessary if all potential group members have already joined the action. To join the group, a potential member who meets the requirements must submit a written declaration to a group representative. Once the designated time limit (no more than three months) expires, the court sets a deadline for the defendant to raise objections concerning the participation of the members in the group or subgroups. In monetary claims, the burden of proof regarding group membership lies with the claimant, while in other claims, it is sufficient for group membership to be presumed (Article 16). After the defendant's deadline has passed, the court determines who comprises the group. In its decision, the court specifies the names of the group members. The court's decision regarding group composition is also appealable. Once it becomes final, opting out is not permitted.

In the third part of the proceedings, the court adjudicates on the merits of the case. The proceedings ends with a judgment in which the court either rules in favour of the claim or denies it in whole or in part, stating that it is not legitimate. At this stage, the court also issues a decision on the costs of the proceedings. According to the Act on Group Proceedings, the agreement between the attorney and the claimant may take the form of contingency fees, with a maximum amount of 20% of the award granted by the court to the claimant (Article 5).[8]

A final court judgement, mentioning the group members and the value of their claims, is subject to execution as a title for pecuniary performance (Article 22). In case of non-pecuniary performance, a group representative (a group member, Financial Ombudsman, municipal/regional consumer ombudsman) or a qualified entity, is entitled to apply for commencement of execution. In case of court judgements on injunctions, when the defendant does not comply with the judgement, the court may issue a decision on penalties (Article 23 b).

8 Poland is one of few examples of countries in Europe expressly allowing for contingency fees in group proceedings: see Tulibacka (2024: 740).

3.2 Data and analysis

One can assume that with nearly 15 years of operation, Poland has accumulated sufficient experience thus far to reflect on the functioning of the law of group proceedings. According to general statistical information from the Ministry of Justice, there were 319 collective claims submitted to the district courts in Poland from 2013 to 2021. However, while the number of claims submitted to the courts appears promising, only a fraction of those cases has been admissible for group proceedings and just a few cases reached the final phase of proceedings in which the court decided on the merits.

3.2.1 Collective action in numbers

As a starting point, it needs to be clarified that the number of collective claims mentioned above does not correspond to the number of proceedings initiated. The data reflects the total number of collective claims submitted to all relevant courts. It includes information about the claims that were (i) returned due to formal deficiencies, (ii) rejected for not meeting the formal requirements for group proceedings, and (iii) denied because they lost the case. By the end of 2021, 63 cases remained, and we cannot confirm whether the group proceedings have been instituted.

The aforementioned data suggests that from 2010 to 2021, 135 cases reached the final phase of proceedings in which the court decided on the merits.[9] My research conducted at the District Court in Warsaw confirmed that this assumption is incorrect. The main reason for the discrepancy between the statistics from the Ministry of Justice and actual court practice is the recurring issue of changing court file numbers. For statistical purposes, each collective claim is counted as a separate case; however, practice shows that many of these court files pertain to the same case. This is due to several factors. Firstly, some collective claims are returned by the court due to formal deficiencies. As a result of correcting these formal defects (such as most likely payment of court fees), the same collective claims are resubmitted to the same court but are registered under a different file number. Secondly, some collective claims are rejected by the court of first instance because they do not meet the formal requirements for group proceedings. Since the court's decision is appealable, claims may be admitted to group proceedings by the second instance court. In such cases, the claims are again submitted to the same court of first instance

9 This number results from the following calculation: 319-69-52-63= 135. 319 collective claims in total; 69 group actions returned; 52 group actions rejected; 63 actions remaining (i.a. not being processed by the court so far).

Table 3.1 Collective claims in civil cases (court files C) in district courts in first instance submitted between 2010 and 2021

Year	*Brought*	*Processed*				
		Altogether[1]	*Including*			*Remaining*
			Rejected	*Denied*	*Returned*	
2010	21	.	.	.	.	.
2011	37	21	4		11	20
2012	35	20	6	**1**	10	33
2013	22	26	5	**6**	5	29
2014	41	19	9	**2**	7	51
2015	32	31	9	**2**	7	52
2016	30	23	5	**2**	10	59
2017	16	27	6	**3**	4	48
2018	22	18	1	**4**		52
2019	16	25	1	**2**	8	43
2020	19	15	2		4	47
2021	28	12	4	**1**	3	63
IN TOTAL	**319**	**237**	**52**	**23**	**69**	

Source: Statistical information of the Polish Ministry of Justice[2]

1 **The column "altogether" represents all cases that have been processed in the given year. It does not inlude only rejected, returned or denied claims, but also claims that were settled in court or out-of-court, adjudicated for the benefit of claimant, or cases supended, for example, because of the bancrupcy of the defendant.**

2 Ministerstwo Sprawiedliwości, Wydział Statystyki i Analiz, Opracowania wieloletnie.

and are once more registered under a different file number. Thirdly, the same situation occurs when the proceedings are stayed after the commencement date (for example, due to the bankruptcy of the defendant). If the claim is resubmitted, it also receives a different court file number.

Consequently, research shows that in practice, the same collective actions are registered under different court file numbers, and therefore, the analysis of the statistical information of the Ministry of Justice only is insufficient to assess the reality of collective redress in Poland.

3.2.2 Register of group proceedings

In 2017, an amendment to the Act on Group Proceedings established a register of group proceedings overseen by the Ministry of Justice.[10] This register contains information about group proceedings that are still pending as well

10 2017 Amendment to the Act on Pursuing Claims in Group Proceedings, Journal of Laws 2018 item 573.

as those in which the court has made a decision on the merits. Its purpose is to provide information for potential group members who wish to opt in to pending or future group proceedings.[11] Additionally, the information on final judgments included in the register could be useful for individuals who could have been group members but did not receive the correct information about pending proceedings. By examining historical court decisions, potential group members could compare their claims with the court's findings and evaluate their chances of success in potential future group actions.

Contrary to expectations, the register has minimal (if any) value in practice and does not meet the needs of potential group members. The primary reason for this failure is that the register is not updated and, therefore, is not utilised by its target audience. It is difficult to determine whether the delays in updates to the register are due to the courts failing to provide information to the Ministry of Justice in a timely manner or whether the authority itself is slow to add the information into the system. In practice, information about pending and future proceedings, which is vital for potential group members, is primarily distributed by attorneys representing consumers.[12] Overall, potential group members are often unaware that a register of group proceedings exists in Poland.

The register of group proceedings includes information about proceedings initiated on or after 1 June 1 2017. It does not account for historical proceedings that began before this date, which certainly limits the register's applicability. This is quite disappointing considering that group proceedings in Poland tend to be lengthy (many proceedings started before 1 June 2017 are still ongoing) and that the overall number of group proceedings is relatively low. From a claimant's perspective, it would be extremely beneficial to include all proceedings initiated under the Act on Group Proceedings in the register. Having a complete overview would facilitate the assessment of the likelihood of success for future claims.

Furthermore, the register must include information required by the court to publish the decision regarding the commencement of group proceedings. This information includes, among other things, the subject matter of the case. In practice, this requirement is interpreted differently by those responsible for submitting information to the register of group proceedings. For instance, the register references the case file no. I C 7/21 that was initiated before the district court in Opole, which concerns financial claims. Unfortunately, there is no information available about the details of this case. Despite the fact that this case was concluded by a final court judgment, this judgment has not been published, and it is impossible to obtain information about the submitted

11 Justification for the proposal of the 2017 amendment to the Act on Group Proceedings, pp. 88–89.

12 An excellent portal dedicated to class actions in Poland (in English language also) is run by one of the Polish law firms leading in group proceedings: https://classaction.pl/en/homepage.

claim. If the purpose of the register is to inform potential claimants about pending or concluded proceedings for future similar claims, it is essential to expand the scope of the register and include information about the details of the case.

There is a significant disparity in the number of collective actions submitted to the Polish district courts. Some courts have never adjudicated cases in group proceedings, while others have a notable number of group actions.[13] Currently, there are records of 15 district courts with a total of 47 group proceedings (pending or closed). This indicates that more than two-thirds of Polish district courts, which are responsible for adjudicating group proceedings, have never encountered such cases.[14] Some courts handled only one collective proceedings within this 15-year time-span. The highest number of collective proceedings is initiated at the District Court in Warsaw, with a total of 21 group proceedings.

3.3 Group proceedings before the District Court in Warsaw

Compared to other Polish district courts, the number of collective claims submitted to the District Court in Warsaw (in Polish: *Sąd Okręgowy w Warszawie*) is significant. Between 2013 and 2020, a total of 80 collective claims were submitted there. For this research, I obtained a list of all 80 court files registered as a result of collective claims submitted to the District Court in Warsaw with the aim of conducting an empirical study.[15] However, during the research process, it became clear that some of the court files were not available.[16] Eventually, I was granted access to 75 court files registered as a result of collective claims. These court files constituted the primary research sample, which was further complemented by information gathered during consultations with different institutions and stakeholders engaged in group proceedings. The list of respondents included municipal (regional) consumer ombudsmen submitting group actions, representatives of the Financial Ombudsman (*Rzecznik Finansowy*), the Polish Commissioner for Human Rights (*Rzecznik Praw Obywatelskich*) representatives of the President

13 Currently there are 47 district courts in Poland competent for adjudicating cases in group proceedings in thefirst instance, see: Regulation of the Polish Ministry of Justice as of 28.12.2018 on establishing seats andjurisdictions of the courts of appeal, district courts and regional courts and the scope of adjudication, (Journal of Laws 2021 item 1269 with amendments).

14 https://www.gov.pl/web/sprawiedliwosc/lista-sadow-okregowych ; access (10.10.2023).

15 Annex no. 1 to this book: List of case files for group proceedings pending and/or closed between 01.01.2013-30.06.2020 before the District Court in Warsaw

16 One court file was flooded with water, two court files were borrowed from another court, and one court file was used by the judge.

of UOKIK, and leading Polish attorneys representing the parties in group proceedings.

In the study, I examined 75 court files registered due to collective claims submitted to the District Court in Warsaw. The aim of these claims was to initiate group proceedings in accordance with the Act on Group Proceedings. It turns out that 10 out of the 75 cases were returned to the claimants due to formal deficiencies. Consequently, 65 civil law cases were initiated as a result of these collective claims. However, this number does not reflect the total group proceedings that were instituted before the District Court in Warsaw. Only 30 collective claims were certified by this court as admissible for group proceedings, and some of them are still pending.

It is essential to understand that from 2013 to 2020, the District Court in Warsaw adjudicated only eleven group proceedings on their merits. Among these, six judgements resulted in the denial of claims, while five judgements favoured the claimants. In the following, I present an overview of the cases under consideration to discuss the course of these proceedings and to identify some practical obstacles that impede effective collective redress.

3.3.1 Cases denied

The District Court in Warsaw denied collective claims in the following cases.

3.3.1.1 Case I C 599/14—*'OFE'*

This case was initiated in 2014 against the State Treasury and several pension companies.[17] It involved damages related to the transfer of funds from the so-called Open Pension Fund (in Polish: *Otwarty Fundusz Emerytalny*, OFE) to the Social Security Fund (in Polish: *Fundusz Ubezpieczeń Społecznych*, FUS). The group, consisting of more than 50 members, was represented by one of its members. The claimant sought a declaration of the invalidity of the legal act of redeeming funds accumulated in OFE accounts, which stemmed from the legal obligation to transfer funds from the OFE to the FUS. After the claim was filed, in 2015 the Polish Constitutional Court ruled that the cancellation of savings in OFE, resulting from an amendment to the Law on Open Pension Funds, is compliant with the Polish Constitution.[18]

Compared to other cases, this one was handled very effectively by the court: in 2015, it issued a decision to certify the case for group proceedings; in 2016, it ordered an announcement in the press; in 2017, it determined the composition of the group; and in 2018, it adjudicated on the merits, denying the claim. The court referenced the decision of the Polish Constitutional

17 Judgment of the District Court in Warsaw of 14.02.2018, file no. I C 599/14, POSP.
18 Judgment of the Polish Constitutional Tribunal, 4.11.2015, file no. K 1/14.

Tribunal and stated that funds derived from insurance premiums are public funds, not private savings of the insured individuals. This was justified by the fact that these funds came from the obligatory and universal pension contribution, which has a public character. The court agreed with the defendants' arguments that the redemption of 51% of the settlement units and their transfer to the FUS were not legal but rather technical and organisational in nature, leading *de facto* to a temporary change in the entity administering public funds. In this sense, in the court's opinion, there was no expropriation in this case; there was no prejudice on the part of the insured, regardless of the amount of pension benefit paid in the future.

3.3.1.2 Case I C 1281/15—*'Bank Millennium'*

The most remarkable group proceedings in Poland so far is the case against Bank Millenium. The significance of this case can be justified for at least two reasons: the size of the group—more than 5,000 consumers opted in—and the duration of the proceedings; it has been pending for 10 years already.[19] In 2014, the Municipal Consumer Ombudsman in Olsztyn, acting as a group representative, filed a lawsuit to confirm the bank's liability for unjust enrichment resulting from the collection of excessively high loan instalment amounts from group members. The amount of these instalments was calculated according to the provisions of the agreements based on a contract form containing abusive clauses regarding the indexation of the loan amount granted and its repayment instalments to the Swiss franc exchange rate. According to the claimant, the unjust enrichment was caused by the application of an abusive clause, which allowed the defendant to charge the group members higher amounts for loan repayment. The claimant argued that the case met the criteria for group proceedings, asserting that each group member has claims of the same kind, based on the same or a similar factual basis. It further contended that each member of the group entered into an agreement based on the same abusive indexation clause (which was confirmed by a judgment from the Court of Competition and Consumer Protection, SOKiK), subsequently entered into the register of abusive clauses.[20]

In 2015 the District Court in Warsaw rejected the lawsuit due to the lack of 'the same or the same factual basis of the claim.'[21] The Court of Appeal in Warsaw amended its decision and declined to dismiss the lawsuit, stating that the district court unjustifiably treated the factual basis of the claim as encompassing all circumstances necessary to determine the merits of the

19 Judgment of the District Court in Warsaw of 24.05.2022, file no. I C 1281/15, not published, not final.

20 Judgment of SOKiK of 14.12.2010, file no. XVII Amc 426/09.

21 Decision of the District Court in Warsaw of 28.05.2015, file no. I C 691/14.

claim judgment.[22] The proceedings were very lengthy due to the procedural errors that occurred during the process. For instance, the District Court in Warsaw did not rule on the admissibility of group proceedings within the time frame specified in the Code of Civil Procedure but did so during a closed-door hearing. Additionally, the court did not hold a mandatory hearing before issuing a judgment. As a result of numerous complaints, the composition of the group was not determined until 2019. The case received support from various institutions—in 2021, the Polish Commissioner for Human Rights joined the case, followed by the Financial Ombudsman in 2023.

In 2022, the court of first instance adjudicated on the merits and denied the claim. Surprisingly, it found that the indexation clauses in the loan agreements were not abusive. In particular, it stated that

> in the opinion of the adjudication panel, the claimant did not prove that the provisions of the Group Members' loan agreements, which contain the same regulations, shape their rights and obligations as consumers in a manner that is contrary to good practices, grossly violating their interests. […] The fact that the exchange rate used to convert the due loan installment for repayment was determined by the Respondent's employees does not necessarily imply that it was arbitrary. This is because the claimant has not provided adequate evidence to support this allegation, aside from a mere assertion. Meanwhile, to prove the thesis that the defendant determined (shaped) the CHF exchange rate arbitrarily, the plaintiff should indicate—by precisely quoting the rates used by the defendant and comparing them with market rates—that indeed the defendant's rates, along with their fluctuations, do not align with market indications, i.e., deviate from them to such an extent that they can be considered arbitrary manner.

The reasoning the District Court in Warsaw mentioned above clearly contradicts the interpretation of the provisions of Directive 93/13 on unfair terms in consumer contracts made by the Court of Justice of the European Union (CJEU).[23] The CJEU emphasises that

> the content of a clause in a loan agreement must enable a consumer who is reasonably well-informed and reasonably observant and circumspect to understand, based on clear and intelligible criteria, how the foreign currency exchange rate used to calculate the amount of the repayment installments is set, so that the consumer can determine at any time the exchange rate applied by the seller or supplier.

22 Decision of the Court of Appeal in Warsaw of 21.09.2015, file no. I Acz 1648/15.

23 Judgment of the Court of Justice of the EU of 18.11.2021, C-212/20, *M.B.* and *B.P. v. "A."*, ECLI:EU:C:2021:934.

In light of this judgment, a general reference to market value or other generic clauses is insufficient. Notably, the latest case law from the Polish Supreme Court also aligns with this perspective of the Court of Justice. The Supreme Court has determined that the unilateral determination of the foreign currency exchange rate by the bank,[24] without reference to objective criteria, is contrary to the nature of the legal relationship in a loan indexed to foreign currency. This confirms that in consumer contracts, provisions regarding abusive clauses should be applied in such situations. The case is still pending before the court of appeal.

3.3.1.3 Case III C 798/15 — *'Spółdzielnia przy Metrze'*

This case was submitted in 2013 by a group representative who entered into an agreement with the cooperative 'Spółdzielnia przy Metrze' for the construction of premises and parking spaces.[25] All group members finalised the agreements according to standard contract terms. As per the agreements, the construction was to be completed by the end of 2009. However, in practice, the premises were handed over at the turn of 2010/2011, and notarial deeds were executed in 2011. In the collective action for payment, the claimant sought damages for lost profits due to the inability to exercise ownership rights over the premises within a specific time frame, attributable to the cooperative's improper contract performance, which resulted in a significant delay in the project's implementation. The damage stemmed from the fact that group members could neither use nor lease their premises.

In 2014, the District Court in Warsaw rejected the claim.[26] However, following an appeal, the judgment was amended in 2015, and the court of appeal found the case admissible for a group proceeding.[27] In 2017, the court determined the composition of the group and in 2019, it denied the claim.[28] It found that claims for damages related to the inability to use the premises cannot be estimated in an approximate manner, regardless of the circumstances of any particular group member. It pointed out that 'the mere fact that a claim is pursued in a group proceeding does not exempt the claimant from proving the amount of damage suffered individually with respect to each member of the groups and subgroups.' The court stated that

> the claims pursued in the present case, despite the formal admissibility of their adjudication in group proceedings, were in fact unsuitable for

24 Resolution of the Polish Supreme Court of 28.04.2022, file no. III CZP 40/22.

25 Judgment of the District Court in Warsaw of 26.04.2019, file no. III C 798/15; Judgment of the Court of Appeal in Warsaw of 26.11.2020, file no. VI Aca 192/20.

26 Decision of the District Court in Warsaw of 19.11.2014, file no. III C 376/13.

27 Decision of the Court of Appeal in Warsaw, file no. VI Acz 479/15.

28 Judgment of the District Court in Warsaw of 26.04.2019, file no. III C 798/15. Judgment of the Court of Appeal in Warsaw of 26.11.2020, file no. VI Aca 192/20.

pursuing under this procedure. This is because admitting the claim would have required the presentation of separate evidence proving that each member of the class suffered damages in an amount dependent on that specific individual's circumstances. In practice, this would mean the necessity of conducting dozens of separate evidentiary proceedings regarding the fact of incurring and the amount of damage, as if the individual claims were pursued in separate proceedings. Thus, conducting the case in group proceedings did not provide the members of the group any advantage over bringing individual actions and may even have been disadvantageous for them, as it deprived them of the opportunity to claim and prove the total amount of the damage suffered.

3.3.1.4 Case XXIV C 339/15—*'Remuneration of the police civil servants'*

Another claim that the court denied was initiated in 2015.[29] A collective action for payment was brought by a representative group that sought damages for the lack of salary valorisation for civil servants in the police since 2009. As the basis for the State Treasury's liability for damages, the claimant cited a tort—specifically, the omission of public authority in the drafting of budget laws from 2011 to 2014. The defendant, however, argued that the lack of salary valorisation was indeed influenced by the budget laws from 2010 to 2014, and that establishing damages would require proving the unconstitutionality of these laws. The District Court in Warsaw certified the claim for group proceedings in 2015, and one year later, it ordered the relevant announcement in the press, while in 2018, the composition of the group was determined.[30] Ultimately, the court denied the claim on the basis that there was no legal obligation to issue a relevant normative act stipulating the valorisation of salaries in the state budget zone at a level exceeding 100%.[31]

3.3.1.5 Case XXV C 250/18—*'Bank BZWBK—Amber Gold pyramid scheme'*

The District Court of Warsaw adjudicated several group actions stemming from one of the largest financial scandals in Poland—the activities of Amber Gold.[32] All of these cases resulted from the same fraud. The company promised to invest clients' money in gold and other precious metals, but it turned out to be a pyramid scheme. This collective action marked the first group

29 Judgment of the District Court in Warsaw of 5.12.2018, file no. XXIV X 339/15 (unpublished).
30 Decision of the Court of Appeal in Warsaw of 11.4.2018, file no. I Acz 147/18.
31 Judgement of the District Court in Warsaw of 5.12.2018, file no. XXIV C 399/15 (unpublished)
32 Among those cases was this case in hand in which the claim was denied, see: Judgment of the District Court in Warsaw of 31.7.2019, file no. XXV C 250/18.

proceedings in which the court evaluated the merits of claims related to Amber Gold's activities. Interestingly, the claimant sought damages not from the company itself, as it was in bankruptcy, but from BZWBK bank, which had been cooperating with Amber Gold. Members of the group were seeking compensation from the defendant bank for damages incurred, among other reasons, due to the bank's failure to comply with its reporting obligations regarding Amber Gold and its continued cooperation with the company despite knowledge of its illegal financial activities. All group members were former clients of the company who voluntarily entrusted substantial funds for precious metals trading. Amber Gold has been listed in the Polish Financial Supervision Authority's (*Komisja Nadzoru Finansowego*, KNF) 'list of public warnings' since 2009. Based on publicly available information, KNF concluded that Amber Gold was highly likely to engage in banking activities without a licence, particularly by accepting deposits in order to expose them to risk.

The respondent maintained bank accounts for Amber Gold from 2009 to 2012 and entered into six agreements for the provision of safe deposit boxes, which, however, were unsuitable for storing larger quantities of gold or other precious metals due to their size. Furthermore, storing precious metals was not part of the services offered by the defendant bank. Amber Gold stated in its advertising materials that precious metals purchased with funds obtained from consumers were stored in safe deposit boxes at the defendant bank. In 2012, the bank terminated Amber Gold's bank account agreement and filed a criminal complaint. The company was declared bankrupt in that year, and the claimant's claims indicate that the group members have not recovered their money paid to Amber Gold. The bankruptcy trustee noted that the claims would be satisfied at most by about 10%.

In May 2015, the District Court in Warsaw certified a claim for group proceedings[33] and in 2018 the composition of the group was determined.[34] In 2019, the court, in a judgment, denied the claim, stating that it was unfounded because the claimant failed to prove all the necessary prerequisites for liability for damages, including the existence of an adequate (direct) causal link between the defendant's act (omission) and the plaintiff's damage. The court also assumed that the defendant's actions (omissions) were not unlawful but merely delayed.[35]

3.3.2 Cases in favour of the claimant

Over last 15 years time-span, there are only six group proceedings in which the District Court in Warsaw ruled in favour of the claimants. These cases are as follows.

33 Decision of the District Court in Warsaw of 2.4.2015, file no. XXV C 148/14.
34 Decision of the District Court in Warsaw of 26.01.2018, file no. XXV C 148/14.
35 Judgement of the District Court in Warsaw of 31.7.2019, file no. XXV C 250/18.

3.3.2.1 Case II C 771/13—*'Travel agency Gromada'*

One of the few examples of consumer success stories in group proceedings is a case initiated in 2013 by a collective action on behalf of 19 consumers for the improper performance of an agreement with a travel services provider.[36] The group representative claimed compensation per capita in the amount of PLN 1,132 for material damage and PLN 2,500 for non-material damage resulting from the non-performance or improper performance of services constituting a package holiday. The consumers participated in a trip to Paris. Upon arrival, it became clear that there was no room for them in a hotel in the centre; as a result, they were accommodated 34 kilometres from the city centre, in a hotel that was not up to the standard of the one they had paid for. The value of the damage, according to the claimant, was determined as the difference between the price of the hotel they paid for and the one in which they were actually accommodated.

In 2014, the court certified the group action for a group proceeding. One year later, it determined the composition of the group. In 2018, the court awarded compensation of PLN 1,800 for each class member (PLN 800 for material damage and PLN 1,000 for non-material damage) and dismissed the claim within the remaining scope. Following the claimant's appeal, the court of appeal amended the judgment and awarded additional damages of PLN 832 to each group member. As a result, consumers received a total of PLN 1132 compensation for material and PLN 1,500 for non-material damage resulted from the improper performance of services that constituted a package holiday.

3.3.2.2 Case II C 222/16—*'AXA'*

The case involved a nationwide scandal that took place a few years ago in Poland concerning the so-called liquidation fees charged by insurers when consumers sought to terminate unit-linked insurance policies.[37] The proceedings against AXA were initiated as a result of one of many collective actions brought against insurers before the District Court in Warsaw, and this case is the only one (out of two total) in which the court of first instance has adjudicated on the merits. A group action, initiated in 2015, focused on establishing AXA's liability for using an abusive contract term that imposed grossly excessive liquidation fees. Such contractual provisions were deemed abusive and were included in the register of prohibited clauses. Consumers were represented by the Municipal Consumer Ombudsman, and their claim was supported by the Financial Ombudsman, who issued a reasoned opinion in the

36 Judgment of the District Court in Warsaw of 29.3.2018., file no. II C 771/13 (unpublished); judgment of Court of Appeal in w Warsaw of 28.06.2019., file no. V ACa 554/18 (unpublished).

37 Judgment of the District Court in Warsaw of 14.12.2020, file no. II C 222/16.

case. This case is discussed in more detail in the section 3.4, of this chapter regarding the institutional support of the Financial Ombudsman.

3.3.2.3 Case XXIV C 554/14—*'Generali'*

A very similar factual circumstance occurred in a group proceeding commenced against another insurer—Generali.[38] The case was instituted as a result of a group action brought by the Municipal Consumer Ombudsman against Generali regarding a grossly excessive liquidation fee unlawfully collected by the company. Similarly to the AXA case, the Financial Ombudsman issued a reasoned opinion relevant to the case. The course of these proceedings is also discussed in details in the section 3, 4, of this chapter regarding institutional support provided by the Financial Ombudsman.

3.3.2.4 Case XXV C 1614/16—*'Liability of the State Treasury for Amber Gold'*

To date, there is only one group action related to the Amber Gold financial scandal in which the court ruled in favour of the former clients of the company.[39] It has already been explained that the company went bankrupt and that no liability of the bank BZWBK was confirmed in the other case. Therefore, in this case, the group members sought compensation for the damage caused by the prosecutor's unlawful failure to fulfil statutory duties from 2010 to 2012. The claimant argued that, despite the fact that starting in 2010, the authority had sufficient evidence that Amber Gold committed a crime, it did not bring charges for more than two years. Unlike other lawsuits filed in connection with the criminal activities of Amber Gold, the group action in question sought to hold the State Treasury liable for the omission of its units under Article 417 par. 1 of the Civil Code in conjunction with Article 415 of the Civil Code, and on this basis sought liability for damages. The claimant asserted that the damage suffered by the group members consisted of the money paid to the company as a deposit and pointed out the causal connection between the damage and the omission. The claimant argued that the group members would not have paid Amber Gold if the prosecution had acted promptly. A total of 164 group members joined this action, seeking payment of more than PLN 21 million in total.

In 2016, after upholding the plaintiff's claim, the Court of Appeal in Warsaw certified the claim for group proceedings. One year later, the composition of the group was determined by the court. After a very complex

38 Judgment of the District Court in Warsaw of 10.05.2017, file no. XXIV C 554/14.
39 Judgment of the District Court in Warsaw of 1.07.2022, file no. XXV C 1614/16 (in appeal).

submission of evidence, the district court ruled in favour of the claimant in 2022. The judgment is not final, and the proceedings before the Court of Appeal in Warsaw is still ongoing.

3.3.2.5 Case III C 603/15—*'Polski Związek Motorowy'*

This case exemplifies a claim ideally suited for group proceedings.[40] A group representative initiated a collective claim for damages against the Polish Motor Association (*Polski Związek Motorowy*) due to improper fulfilment of an obligation related to a ticket sale contract for a sports event (an international speedway race). According to the claimant, the competition was conducted in a manner inconsistent with the standards for hosting a sports event, primarily due to inadequate preparation of the track, which led to the competition ending prematurely. The plaintiff argued that the material damages equalled the price of tickets paid by a group of speedway fans to attend the event. In 2016, the District Court in Warsaw admitted the case to group proceedings, and in 2017, the class composition was established. In 2020, the court ruled in favour of the claimant, awarding compensation to each class member. Although this case had a favourable outcome, it is worth noting that the proceedings lasted a total of five years, and given the low value of the claim, consumers must have been exceptionally determined to pursue this claim in this manner.

3.3.2.6 Case XXV C 318/15 *'Home Broker'*

In 2015, a group action was initiated to establish Home Brokers' liability.[41] The company served as an intermediary in the sale of investment apartments in a hotel located near the Baltic Sea and offered simultaneous leases for the sold apartments (so-called condo investments). Due to the developer's financial issues, the investment was taken over by Idea Bank. Regardless, Home Broker assured its clients of the investment's success, which was ultimately never realised, and the developer eventually declared bankruptcy. The claimant based their claims on the assertion that the defendant employed aggressive sales techniques and failed to disclose information about the developer's situation. In 2017, as a result of an appeal, the Court of Appeal in Warsaw admitted the case for group consideration proceedings.[42] In 2019, the composition of the group—consisting of 29 people—was determined. In 2020, the District Court in Warsaw issued a judgment establishing the defendant's liability; however, due to Home Brokers' bankruptcy, the proceedings were

40 Judgment of the District Court in Warsaw of 17.02.2020, file no. III C 603/15 (in appeal).
41 Judgment of the District Court in Warsaw of 6.11.2020, file no. XXV C 318/15.
42 Decision of the Court of Appeal in Warsaw of 1.3.2017, file no. VI Acz 1461/16.

suspended. Despite the claimant winning the case, the group members were unable to recover their invested funds.

3.4 Institutional support for consumers in group proceedings

Many of the aforementioned collective actions brought before the Warsaw District Court were supported by public authorities. A key example is the support provided by municipal consumer ombudsmen and, more recently, by the Financial Ombudsman, who can act on behalf of consumers as a claimant in group proceedings. Additionally, in some cases, opinions strengthening the claims have been issued by the President of UOKiK and the Polish Commissioner for Human Rights. The following discussion addresses the main competencies of these institutions and provides some evidence-based data on their activities during group proceedings.

3.4.1 Municipal Consumer Ombudsmen

Polish law establishes a distinct framework of several regional consumer ombudsmen (in Polish: *Miejski/Powiatowy Rzecznik Konsumentów*). One of their responsibilities is to assist consumers seeking redress in group proceedings.[43] According to the Act on Group Proceedings, the ombudsman may act as a group representative in consumer claims as a claimant. It is essential that, in such cases, the group is exempt from court fees, which is especially important considering that legal costs are a significant barrier preventing consumers from pursuing claims in court.

It is of a great practical relevance that municipal consumer ombudsman is not obligated to bring actions on behalf of consumers; it is simply her or his prerogative, which she or he does not have to exercise. In practice, different ombudsmen exhibit varying attitudes toward group proceedings. Some tend to agree to assume the role of group representative, while others consistently refuse to engage in any proceedings. This is related not only to the ombudsman's personal beliefs about the appropriateness and success of such litigation but, more importantly, to the personnel and financial resources required to participate in the proceedings. Unfortunately, the institution of the municipal consumer ombudsman in Poland is clearly underfunded and continually lacks sufficient human resources. It should be emphasised that representing consumers in group proceedings is just one of many tasks of this institution.

43 Possibility of bringing court actions on behalf of consumers is only one of many tasks of the Municipal Consumer Ombudsman, see: Article 42 of the ACCP.

Experience shows that since the Act on Group Proceedings came into effect, seven municipal consumer ombudsmen have represented a total of 10,000 consumers in 17 group proceedings. The Municipal Consumer Ombudsman in Warsaw has demonstrated the highest activity, representing consumers in eight group proceedings (two cases against mBank S.A.,[44] one case against Spółdzielnia przy Metrze S.A.,[45] two cases against Towarzystwo Ubezpieczeń na Życie Europa S.A.,[46] one case against Towarzystwo Ubezpieczeń Aegon S.A.,[47] and one case against BZWBK S.A.[48]). Additionally, the Municipal Consumer Ombudsman in Warsaw represented consumers in a case against Getin Noble Bank S.A., where a settlement was reached at the pre-trial stage of proceedings.

Other group proceedings were initiated by the Municipal Ombudsman in Szczecin (four cases against Skandia Życie Towarzystwo Ubezpieczeń S.A.[49] and AXA Życie Towarzystwo Ubezpieczeń S.A.[50]), the Municipal Ombudsman in Olsztyn (two cases against Bank Millenium S.A.[51]), the Municipal Ombudsman in Poznań (one case against Getin Noble Bank S.A.[52]), the Municipal Ombudsman in Kołobrzeg (one case against Open Life Towarzystwo Ubezpieczeń na Życie S.A.[53]), the Muncipal Ombudsman in Pruszków (one case against Generali Życie Towarzystwo Ubezpieczeń S.A.[54]) and the Municipal Ombudsman in Szczecinek (one case against Bank BPH S.A.[55]). The subject matter of these cases primarily involved consumer disputes related to financial services, brought against the insurance companies and banks.

44 Group proceedings before the District Court in Łódź, file no. I C 1219/20 (previously I C 519/16); group proceedings before the District Court in Łódź, file no. II C 1693/10.

45 Group proceedings before the District Court in Warsaw, file no. III C 976/12.

46 Group proceedings before the District Court in Warsaw, file no. I C 464/16; group proceedings before the District Court in Warsaw, file no. XXIV C 709/15.

47 Group proceedings before the District Court in Warsaw, file no. III C 1322/13.

48 Group proceedings before the District Court in Wrocław, file no. I C 976/17.

49 Group proceedings before the District Court in Warsaw, file no. XXIV C 500/14 and file no. III 62/14.

50 Group proceedings before the District Court in Warsaw, file no. XXV C 915/14; Group proceedings before the District Court in Warsaw, file no. II C 222/16 and in appeal and before the Court of Appeal in Warsaw, file no. VACa 444/21.

51 Group proceedings before the District Court in Warsaw, file no. IV C 1348/19 and in appeal before the Court of Appeal in Warsaw, file no. V ACz 557/20; Group proceedings before the District Court in Warsaw I C 1281/15 and in appeal before the Court of Appeal in Warsaw, file no. I ACa 599/23.

52 Group proceedings before the District Court in Warsaw, file no. XXV C 1575/15 and in appeal before the Court of Appeal in Warsaw, file no. IV Acz 785/18.

53 Group proceedings before the District Court in Warsaw, file no. XXV C 461/18.

54 Group proceedings before the District Court in Warsaw, file no. XXIV C 554/14 and in appeal before the Court of Appeal in Warsaw, file no. I ACa 1690/17.

55 Group proceedings before the District Court in Gdańsk, file no. XV C 871/18.

3.4.2 Financial Ombudsman (former Insurance Ombudsman)

Institutional support for consumers in group proceedings provided by the Financial Ombudsman is a novel development in Polish law. In 2023, this authority was granted the right to represent consumers in group proceedings initiated as a result of claims against financial market service providers. It is expected that this institution will assume the role previously played by Municipal Consumer Ombudsmen in this area. Since the Financial Ombudsman's authority is relatively new, it has only initiated two collective actions.[56] The District Court in Warsaw rejected the first case because the defendant had no judicial capacity—the Financial Ombudsman sued the Polish branch of a foreign trader.[57] There is no court decision on the certification of the second case so far—the proceedings is still pending. So far, the Financial Ombudsman is the only public authority recognised as a qualified entity entitled *ex lege* to bring consumer representative actions within RAD.

Additionally, the Financial Ombudsman possesses experience in supporting consumers pursuing claims in this manner because it is entitled to express a reasoned opinion (or so-called 'important view') in consumer cases—both in individual and group proceedings. Practice indicates that, although the Financial Ombudsman's opinions are not binding on the court, their expert nature makes them important substantive and supportive material for the courts.[58]

In the subsequent years of the Financial Ombudsman's activity, one can observe a steady increase in the number of requests for important views submitted by the claimants.[59] Interest in this form of institutional support is especially evident in cases involving loans denominated or indexed to the Swiss franc. However, it should be noted that the vast majority of positions were expressed by the Financial Ombudsman during individual proceedings rather than group proceedings. To date, the entity has exercised its authority to express its position in cases involving claims brought in group proceedings only a few times. Most of the significant views issued in these proceedings concerned claims arising from contracts made with insurance companies, with only one view expressed for the purposes of a pending group proceeding

56 The first collective action was brought by the Financial Ombudsman against TF Bank AB S.A. in Warsaw, see:https://rf.gov.pl/komunikat-rzecznika-finansowego-w-sprawie-wniesienia-pierwszego-pozwu-grupowego-przeciwko-tf-bank-ab-s-a-w-sprawie-kredytowania-za kupu-pomp-ciepla/; and the second collective action wasbrought by the Financial Ombudsman against Noble Securities S.A., see: https://archiwum.rf.gov.pl/2024/02/02/rzecznik-finansowy -sklada-powodztwo-w-postepowaniu-grupowym-przeciwko-noble-securities-s-a/. (access: 10.10.2024).

57 Representative action was rejected by the District Court in Warsaw, file no. I C 31/24.

58 Jurkowska-Zeidler (2018: 35).

59 Reports on the activity of the Financial Ombudsman in 2015–2022 are available online: https://rf.gov.pl/o-nas/sprawozdania/ (access 10.10.2023).

against a bank acting as a defendant.[60] Seven group proceedings in which the Financial Ombudsman issued an important view ended in favour of the claimant, either by judgment[61] or settlement.[62] It is noteworthy that in all of these cases, the groups were represented by the Municipal Consumer Ombudsman, who requested the Financial Ombudsman issue an important view in those instances.

Of all the group proceedings during which the Financial Ombudsman expressed a reasoned opinion on the case, only two have been adjudicated on the merits by the court so far. Both proceedings were initiated before the District Court in Warsaw and involved claims arising from contracts with insurance companies.

One of those cases was brought against Axa Życie Towarzystwo Ubezpieczeń S.A. by the Municipal Consumer Ombudsman in Szczecin, representing a group of 31 consumers. The collective action concerned the contractual clauses specifying the rules for determining the amount of the fee charged to group members in the event of the termination of insurance contracts. The claimant sought a determination that the insurance company was unauthorised to charge such fees and thus that the clauses shall not be binding on the group members.[63] According to the Financial Ombudsman, which presented its position in the case to the court, the provisions of the general terms and conditions of the agreements used by AXA and covered by the lawsuit, which set the amount of the liquidation fee, shaped the rights and obligations of consumers in a way that contradicts good practice and significantly infringes upon consumer rights interests.[64] Furthermore, according to the Financial Ombudsman, the potential for concluding insurance contracts with an investment component cannot justify a practice where a life insurance contract lacks a protective element, such as a guarantee of a specific benefit in the event of an insurance occurrence. The court of first instance concurred with the group members, stating that the provisions of the models, under which AXA claimed the right to retain a portion of the consumers' savings upon policy termination, constituted abusive contractual provisions and those clauses are not binding on the group members.[65]

60 District Court in Gdańsk, file no. I C 280/18; reasonable opinion no. RF/WBK/POG/630/2018.

61 Judgement of the District Court in Warsaw of 14.12.2020, file no. II C 222/16 ('AXA') and judgement of the District Court in Warsaw of 10.05.2017, file no. XXIV C 554/14 ('Generali).

62 Settlement of 11.12.2019, case file no. III C 62/14 ('Skandia 1'); settlement of 21.05.2020, case file no. XXIV C 500/14 ('Skandia 2); settlement of 17.02.2015, case file no. III C 1322/13, ('Aegon'); settlement of 23.10.2023, case file no. I C 464/16 ('TU na życie EUROPA 1'); settlement of 23.10.2023, case file no. XXIV C 709/15 ('TU na życie Europa 2').

63 The course of the proceedings is described in details by the claimant's attorney: https://lwb.com.pl/i/axa-pozew-o-ustalenie/ (access 10.10.2023).

64 Opinion of the Financial Ombudsman of 30.12.2015.

65 Judgment of the District Court in Warsaw of 14.12.2020, file no. II C 222/16.

The second group action where the court of first instance considered the Financial Ombudsman's position involved the insurance company Generali.[66] The Municipal Consumer Ombudsman in Pruszków initiated a group action for the reimbursement of amounts collected from group members by the defendant without a legal basis, referred to as a 'buyout fee.' The group members were individuals who had entered into life insurance contracts based on the general terms and conditions developed and used by the defendant. Upon termination, the insurer redeemed the units of the accumulated accounts and calculated the policy's value, which was then deducted by an excessively high redemption fee. At the claimant's request, the Insurance Ombudsman (the predecessor of the Financial Ombudsman) submitted a reasoned opinion in the case, stating that the provisions of the agreements were identical in content to those listed in the register of abusive practices clauses.[67] The court ruled in favour of the claimant and awarded the amounts sought by the 165 group members concerning improperly collected redemption fees.[68] The court of appeals upheld the judgment in favour of consumers and dismissed Generali's appeal in its entirety, stating that there was no doubt about the abusive nature of the buyout fee provisions.[69]

Opinions of the Financial Ombudsman (or formerly the Insurance Ombudsman) containing a significant view on the matter also contributed to settlements reached with insurance companies in the following group proceedings, which were pending before the District Court in Warsaw:

- File no. III C 62/14, '*Skandia*' settlement of 11.12.2019;
- File no. XXIV C 500/14, '*Skandia*' settlement of 21.05.2020;
- File no. III C 1322/13, '*Aegon*' settlement of 17.2.2015;
- File no. XXIV C 709/15, '*TU na życie EUROPA*', settlement of 26.10.2023;
- File no. I C 464/16, '*TU na życie EUROPA*', settlement of 26.20.2023.

The content of the settlements is not disclosed to the public.

3.4.3 President of UOKiK

If a collective claim involves consumer protection and the case concerns public interest, the President of UOKiK may present 'standpoint material to the case' (in Polish: *istotny pogląd w sprawie*). This standpoint may be submitted either *ex officio* or at the request of a party. The authority has the discretion to

66 The course of the proceedings is described in detail by the claimant's attorney: https://lwb.com.pl/i/generali-pozew-o-zaplate-1/
67 Opinion of the Insurance Ombudsman, file no. RU/POG/51/AG/14.
68 Judgment of the District Court in Warsaw of 10.05.2017 file no. XXIV C 554/14.
69 Judgment of the Court of Appeal in Warsaw of 6.11.2018,f file no. SA I ACa 1690/17.

decide whether it will participate in the ongoing case by issuing its opinion. If it declines to provide an opinion on the case, the parties have no means to appeal, nor do they have any legal remedies that could compel the authority to present such an opinion. The President of UOKiK operates independent of the parties involved in the dispute. In practice, the authority's position significantly supports consumers in pursuing claims through collective actions.

The President of UOKiK has exercised its authority to issue a substantive view in group proceedings cases several times so far. It is worth noting that the authority expressed its position in Poland's first group action case brought by the Municipal Consumer Ombudsman in Warsaw, representing a group of 1,247 consumers in a dispute against mBank S.A.[70] The lawsuit sought to establish that the bank was liable for damages to consumer-borrowers, which was allegedly due to the bank's improper performance of the agreements. This involved the bank charging borrowers higher loan interest rates than if it had done so correctly. As a result of pending proceedings, the District Court in Łódź[71] followed by the Court of Appeal in Łódź,[72] held that the bank was liable for damages to consumers. Following the bank's cassation, the Supreme Court ruled that the variable loan rate clause challenged by customers was an illegal provision, but only regarding the part specifying the possibility of changing the interest rate.[73] The rest of the clause, concerning the dependence of the interest rate on financial parameters, was not deemed abusive according to the Supreme Court.

The President of UOKiK presented standpoint material to the case and pointed out that the ruling adopted by the Supreme Court violates the provisions of Directive 93/13 on unfair terms and does not take into account case law from the Court of Justice of the European Union. The President of UOKiK held that the disputed contractual provision, which should be regarded as abusive in its entirety, is not binding on consumers *ex lege* and *ex tunc*. The case was pending for almost ten years, and it ended with the bank withdrawing an appeal of the judgment of the court of the first instance.

Other group proceedings in which the President of UOKiK expressed a significant view include the cases against TU Życie Europa pending before the Warsaw District Court: case file no. I C 464/16[74] and case file XXIV C 709/15.[75] Both cases have been dismissed due to the settlement reached by the parties in 2023.

70 Opinion of the President of UOKiK of 29.07.2016, file no. DDK-664-505/16/MF included in the case pending before the Court of Appeal in Łódź, file no. I ACa 1058/15.

71 Judgment of the District Court in Łódź of 3.7.2013, file no. II C 1693/10.

72 Judgment of the Court of Appeal in Łódź of 30.4.2014, file no. I Aca 1209/13 and file no. I Acz 1424/13.

73 Judgment of the Supreme Court of 14.05.2015, file no. II CSK 768/14.

74 Opinion of the President of UOKiK of 30.03.2021, file no. RKT.644.92.2019.AR.

75 Opinion of the President of UOKiK of 11.03.2020, file no. DZOIK-4.664.13.2020.MJ.

3.4.4 Commissioner for Human Rights

Due to legislative changes in civil procedural law that went into effect in 2019, the Commissioner for Human Rights, with the powers of a prosecutor, can also participate in group proceedings.[76] So far, the Commissioner has exercised this right twice—in the cases mentioned above, brought by the Municipal Consumer Ombudsman in Warsaw against mBank[77] and Millenium Bank.[78] These cases have already been discussed in this chapter—the first one in the section regarding the support of the President of UOKiK and the second one in the section regarding cases denied by the District Court in Warsaw.

As a side note, it needs to be recalled that both group proceedings mentioned above related to the consequences of the so-called foreign currency loan crisis. In brief, this problem related to unfair contract terms in consumer loans. This issue was addressed differently in particular Member States. In Poland, no legislative measures have been taken to assist affected consumers sufficiently. The scale of the problem was massive—it was estimated that approximately 550,000 borrowers in Poland were affected. As a result, consumers started court actions against the banks, invoking that the loan contract terms are unfair due to the fact that the indexing mechanism allowed the bank to arrange the exchange rate at its discretion. The national courts were supposed to evaluate whether the terms included in consumer loans shall be assessed in line with requirements specified in Directive 93/13 on unfair terms and consequently, in case of the breach of the fairness requirement, to adjudicate on relevant remedies.[79]

The scale of the problem and its social consequences for borrowers prompted the active support of many institutions. One such initiative was a 'Consumer Forum' established by the Commissioner for Human Rights, comprised of leading Polish consumer law experts. Among its various tasks, the Consumer Forum advised the Commissioner for Human Rights and prepared expert opinions to assist consumers in pursuing claims not only in the aforementioned group proceedings but also in many landmark individual cases that resulted in preliminary rulings from the Court of Justice of the European Union. The Consumer Forum stopped operating but the issue persists, and currently, Poland's Ministry of Justice is working on simplifying foreign currency loan settlements and related court cases.

76 Act of 15 July 1987 on Human Rights Commissioner, (Journal of Laws 2024, No. 1264), Article 14 (4).

77 Opinion of the Human Rights Commissioner of 30.06.2020, file no. V.511.126.2020.MT.

78 Opinion of the Human Rights Commissioner of 14.04.2021, file no. V.510.212.2017.MT.

79 Mucha (2025:14).

3.5 Implementation of RAD in Poland

One might wonder whether the implementation of RAD will significantly transform the landscape of group proceedings in Poland. While final conclusions are premature, several observations can be drawn at this stage. Firstly, the process itself was challenging, and Poland faced significant delays. After multiple governmental proposals for its implementation, RAD was ultimately transposed into national law through the Act of 24 July 2024, which amends the Act on Group Proceedings,[80] and came into effect on 29 August 2024 (hereinafter referred to as the 'Act Amending the Act on Group Proceedings'). Requirements for qualified entities are specified by the Act of 16 February 2007 on Competition and Consumer Protection[81] (hereinafter referred to as 'the ACCP'). Additionally, provisions regarding costs of consumer representative actions are included in the Act of 28 July 2005 on Court Costs in Civil Cases.[82]

Considering that Poland's collective redress system has been in operation for several years, there has been extensive discussion on how to integrate the existing mechanisms with the instruments of representative action provided in RAD. Three implementation scenarios that allow for one-stop-shop proceedings have been considered in Poland.[83] The first model was court-based and private enforcement, in which the President of UOKiK is recognised as one of the qualified entities entitled to bring representative action before the court. The second scenario was founded on an administrative public enforcement model, where the President of UOKiK has the authority to seek both injunctions and compensation. The third option considered was a parallel model: an administrative approach for injunctions and a court-based model for both injunctions and compensation.

In the Act amending the Act on Group Proceedings, the third scenario has been selected. Consequently, a complex framework for enforcing consumer collective interests is created, consisting of three elements:

1. Public enforcement: consists of administrative proceedings (injunctions in the public interest) instituted by the President of UOKiK, in accordance with the Act on Competition and Consumer Protection. As a result of these proceedings, the authority may decide on injunction

80 Act of 24 July 2024 amending the Act on Pursuing Claims in Group Proceedings and Other Laws, (Journal of Laws 2024 No. 1237).

81 Act of 16 February 2007 on Competition and Consumer Protection, (Journal of Laws, 2007, No. 50, Item 331with further amendments), hereinafter referred to as "the ACCP."

82 Act of 28 July 2005 on Court Costs in Civil Cases, (Journal of Laws, 2005 No. 167 Item 1398 with further amendments).

83 Jagielska (2019: 39), Mucha (2019: 18).

and additionally, oblige the trader to pay so called public compensation towards consumers.[84]

2. Private enforcement: involves group proceedings (compensatory redress) initiated by a group member, Municipal Consumer Ombudsman, or Financial Ombudsman, based on the Act on Group Proceedings.
3. Private enforcement, with a public 'twist': representative actions in courts (injunctions and/or compensation) initiated by qualified entities registered with the President of UOKiK, in accordance with the Act Amending the Act on Group Proceedings, which implements RAD.[85]

This structure is quite confusing from both the business and consumer perspectives. It suggests that actions for injunction may be initiated *ex officio* by the President of UOKiK (according to the first option in the list above - as part of administrative proceedings) or by a representative entity on behalf of a group of consumers (as outlined in the third option in the list above above - in civil proceedings before the courts).

In essence, the implementation of RAD does not alter the four-stage course of group proceedings (certification, group formation, proceedings regarding the substance of the case, and enforcement). Instead, it either adds additional requirements that must be met to initiate a representative action or indicates that specific other requirements shall not apply. The most significant changes relate to the scope of collective actions, the requirements for claim certification, recognition of representative entities and third-party funding.

3.5.1 Extended scope of group proceedings

Implementing RAD inevitably extends the scope of group proceedings under Polish law. According to Article 1, section 2 of the Act on Group Proceedings, collective actions may be initiated for product liability claims, tort liability claims, liability for non-performance or improper performance of a contract, and unjust enrichment claims, as well as in all other matters related to consumer claims. The Act excludes claims for the protection of personal interests, except for personal injury claims.

The Act amending the Act on Group Proceedings broadens its scope by incorporating actions for injunctions (to stop trader violations of collective consumer interests) and actions for redress (to remedy trader violations of collective consumer interests), which are later referred to as 'representative actions' within the meaning of RAD. Collective consumer interests are

84 For systematic and competence doubts on public compensation as a measure for remeding the ongoing effects of infringmenet of collective consumer interests in Poland see: Kohutek (2019: 36).

85 Mucha (2024b: 336).

defined as the overall interests of individual consumers and, particularly for the purposes of redress measures, the interests of a group of consumers. A violation of the latter shall be interpreted as a breach of the provisions of EU law outlined in Annex I to RAD. Additionally, it seems that a collective claim could still be submitted by a group member of the Municipal Consumer Ombudsman according to the provisions that refer to 'all consumer claims' if the infringement of collective consumer interests does not relate to any provisions of EU law listed in Annex I to RAD.

3.5.2 Liberalisation of certification requirements

The first stage of group proceedings is the certification of the claim. Article 1, section 1 of the Act on Group Proceedings outlines the criteria for claim admissibility. According to these criteria, collective action must be initiated in the name of at least ten individuals with claims of the same kind and with the same or a similar factual basis. In a rather revolutionary manner, the Act amending the Act on Group Proceedings provides an exception to this rule, stating that in representative actions, claims may also be grounded in the same or a similar legal basis as an alternative to the same or a similar factual basis (Article 1 section 2c). This represents a significant difference because, despite the requirement for the same or a similar factual basis being recognised as one of the most serious obstacles to the efficiency of group proceedings, it was interpreted very strictly by judges adjudicating at the certification stage. It has faced heavy criticism for being overly stringent, formalistic, difficult to implement and, according to some, contrary to the very essence of class action procedure.[86]

Another modification included in the Act amending the Act on Group Proceedings pertains to the requirement that group proceedings may be initiated on behalf of a group of at least ten individuals. The Polish system of group proceedings is based on the opt-in model, where all group members must submit a statement confirming their willingness to join the group. According to the new law, this requirement will not apply to representative actions limited solely to injunctive measures. This is supported by the wording of RAD, which states that for a qualified entity to seek an injunctive measure, individual consumers shall not be obligated to express their desire to be represented by that qualified entity. As a side note, such a provision would not be necessary if Directive 2009/22/EC on injunctions were properly implemented in Poland and if the President of UOKiK were not the sole entity entitled to initiate actions for injunctions.[87] According to the Act amending the Act on Group Proceedings, if a representative action includes both injunctive

86 Tulibacka (2018: 38); Pluskwa- Dąbrowski (2019: 133).
87 Mucha (2019: 13).

and redress measures (a one-stop-shop procedure), the requirement of at least ten members of the group remains in effect.

To enhance the effectiveness of representative actions, the Act amending the Act on Group Proceedings eliminates the so-called commonality requirement concerning monetary claims, which stipulates that collective action is only allowed if the amounts claimed by each group member are equal. According to Article 2, section 3 of the Act on Group Proceedings, if a case involves group members with varying levels of damages, the claim may be limited to declaratory relief only. This requirement significantly restricted the scope of claims. Under the new law, the commonality requirement for monetary claims does not apply to consumer representative actions. This change is both welcome and justified because, in practice, there is twice commonalitys requirement hinders the effective functioning of the procedural mechanism for representative actions, thereby contradicting the goal of RAD.

3.5.3 Recognition of representative entities

Collective action can be initiated on behalf of a group by a group representative—either a group member, a municipal consumer ombudsman, or a Financial Ombudsman. A group representative is a party to the proceedings and, except for a Financial Ombudsman, must be represented by a legal attorney. In addition to the entities mentioned above that can initiate collective action, the Act amending the Act on Group Proceedings permits representative action to be brought by entities registered by the President of UOKiK according to the criteria specified in the new law. It specifies only one authority recognised as a representative entity *ex lege*—namely a Financial Ombudsman—in terms of proceedings initiated on behalf of financial consumers.[88] Surprisingly, under the new law, municipal consumer ombudsmen, which have been the most active organisations in bringing collective actions, are not considered *ex lege* as representative entities within the meaning of RAD.

Moreover, the Act amending the Act on Group Proceedings does not mention any consumer organisation, foundation, or any other public body representing consumer interests in representative actions. Currently, 19 active consumer organisations in Poland are potentially interested in being recognised as representative entities.[89] They are free to decide whether they want to apply for such recognition. At the same time, this entails the risk that, without adequate funding and human resources, consumer organisations and foundations may not be interested in being recognised as representative entities. This seems like quite a likely scenario since in the regulatory impact assessment

88 Some constitutional doubts in this regards have been presented recently, see: Trzaska-Śmieszek, Osmęda (2024: electronic resource).

89 President of UOKiK identified 19 consumer organisations that between 2016 and 2021 applied for funding (subsidy) for their activity in the field of consumer protection.

of the Act amending the Act on Group Proceedings it is stated that introduction of consumer representative actions to Polish law will not incur any additional costs for the national budget being in the disposition of the President of UOKiK.[90] This means that there are currently no additional funds allocated for the operation of consumer organisations as representative entities.

3.5.4 Costs of group proceedings

There are at least three groups of costs that need to be considered when submitting group actions to Polish courts: court fees, attorney's fees and, in the case of representative action, any fees charged by representative entities. The primary principle governing the costs of civil proceedings in Poland is the 'loser pays principle.[91]' This makes group proceedings quite risky, as in cases where the claim is rejected, the claimant must pay not only the court fees but also their own legal representation costs, in addition to those of the defendant.

The national law establishes maximum limits on court fees for civil proceedings. According to the Act on Court Costs in Civil Cases, the fee for a collective action is based on the value of the case and 50% of the fee applicable for monetary claims, but it cannot be less than PLN 100 and cannot exceed PLN 200,000.[92] If non-pecuniary claims are sought, a temporary fee is established at PLN 600. If the value of the claim cannot be determined initially, the temporary fee is set between PLN 300 and PLN 20,000.[93] It is essential that when a collective claim is initiated by the Financial Ombudsman or a municipal consumer ombudsman, group members will not bear court costs.[94] Following the implementation of RAD in Poland, the representative entities recognised as such and registered by the President of UOKiK are also exempt from court fees.[95]

Regarding representative actions as a specific type of group actions, the Act amending the Act on Pursuing Claims in Group Proceedings states that representative entities may request consumers seeking redress measures pay a charge in order to participate in the proceedings. The act specifies a maximum limit of the fee, amounting to up to 5% of the value of the consumer claim, but it also states that it cannot exceed PLN 2,000 for monetary claims and PLN 1,000 for non-pecuniary claims.[96] There is no charge for proceedings

90 Rządowe Centrum Legislacji, *Ocena skutków regulacji projektu ustawy o zmianie ustawy o dochodzeniu roszczeń w postępowaniu grupowym oraz niektórych innych ustaw*, No. UC16, 16.05.2024, https://legislacja.rcl.gov.pl/projekt/12382308/katalog/13040284#13040284 (access 1.09.2024).

91 Piszcz (2017: 237).

92 Article 13d of the Act of 28.7.2005 on Court Costs in Civil Cases, (Journal of Laws 2005 No. 167 Item 1398 with further amendments).

93 Article 15, sec. 2 of the Act on Court Costs in Civil Cases, *op. cit.*

94 Article 96, sec. 1, points 6 and 7 of the Act on Court Costs in Civil Cases, *op. cit.*

95 Article 96, sec. 1, point 7a of the Act on Court Costs in Civil Cases, *op. cit.* (access 1.10.2024).

96 Article 5a of the Act on Pursuing Claims in Group Proceedings, *op. cit.*

initiated by a Financial Ombudsman. In light of the recent amendment, the entry fee is the only cost that should be borne by consumers participating in group proceedings initiated by a representative entity.

In light of the wording of this provision, one might wonder whether consumers participating in representative actions should not bear the costs of attorney's fees. It is not entirely clear, as the Act on Pursuing Claims in Group Proceedings generally allows for contingency fees (success fees) to be paid by group members for their attorney, amounting to up to 20% of the claim awarded to the claimant. The latest amendment does not explicitly exclude this provision from applying to representative actions, and RAD does not disapprove contingency fees as such. However, since the Act on Group Proceedings allows for third-party funding, it could be reasonably expected that attorney's fees may be covered by a third-party funder with an interest in a judgment in favour of the claimant.

3.5.5 Dual role of the President of UOKiK

The implementation of RAD in Poland brings controversies related to the significant role of the President of UOKiK in enforcing consumer law. According to the Act amending the Act on Group Proceedings, the President of UOKiK oversees the entire system of registration and the functioning of representative entities within the private enforcement framework. It is questionable whether government authority should influence and control the entities authorised to submit claims in civil proceedings. Meanwhile, the President of UOKiK remains the sole authority entitled to initiate actions for injunction within the public enforcement path.

The Act amending the Act on Group Proceedings establishes a chaotic system where actions for injunctions related to the same infringement of consumer collective interests by the same trader can be initiated either by the President of UOKiK (in administrative proceedings) or by the representative entity before court. However, there is a clear priority of actions for injunctions brought by the public authority within administrative proceedings over representative actions before the courts. The President of UOKiK recently stated that the latter would complement public enforcement.[97] This mechanism creates a risk that, in the case of a lack of flow of information, the two actions for injunctions against the same trader can be brought simultaneously on both enforcement paths. To avoid such risk, the Act amending the Act of Group Proceedings provides the system in which the representative entity is obliged to notify the President of UOKiK of its intent to bring consumer

97 UOKiK, *Więcej praw dla konsumentów- nowe postępowania grupowe*, electronic resource: https://uokik.gov.pl/wiecej-praw-dla-konsumentow-nowe-postepowania-grupowe. (access 1.10.2024).

representative action for injunction. A representative entity is obliged to provide information about the kind of claim, the trader against which the action will be brought, demands in the statement of claim, as well as circumstances justifying representative action, including a description of the infringement, its duration, the social, economic, or legal consequences of the infringement, and the legal norms the trader infringed. As a result of such notice, within 30 days (or in particularly justified cases 3 months of the notice), the President of UOKiK shall inform the qualified entity whether administrative proceedings for injunction are pending against the same trader committing the same infringement of collective consumer interests. This obligation considerably delays the commencement of the group proceedings by the representative entity and therefore it is questionable whether such restriction is in line with RAD, which provides that national rules should not hamper the effective functioning of representative actions.[98] The reply of the President of UOKiK shall be enclosed by the claimant in the lawsuit seeking action for injunction. In a case when administrative proceedings against the same trader regarding the same infringement of consumer rights is pending, the court shall reject the claim.[99] The representative action shall not be rejected in the case of a one-stop-shop procedure, which is when the qualified entity seeks injunctive and redress measures in one proceeding.

3.5.6 Third-party funding

Implementation of RAD introduces an entirely new solution, previously unknown to the Polish legal system, namely third-party funding.[100] Representative entities may be financed by third parties—derived from fees collected from consumers and traders. The Act on Competition and Consumer Protection specifies that activities of a qualified entity can also be financed by traders, as long as it remains

> independent and not influenced by persons other than consumers, in particular by traders, who have an economic interest in the bringing of any representative action, including in the event of funding by third parties, and, to that end, has established procedures to prevent such influence as well as to prevent conflicts of interest between itself, its funding providers and the interests of consumers.[101]

98 On controversies surrounding the parallel injunction model in Poland, see: Mucha (2024b: 341).
99 Article 10c (1) of the Act on Group Proceedings.
100 Okońska (2024: 50).
101 Article 46f of the ACCP, *op. cit.*

In such cases, the qualified entities must enter into an agreement with the trader or group of traders financing the tasks and the agreement must stipulate the remuneration for the trader. The ACCP provides for a third-party funder a maximum fee of 30% of the claim awarded to the claimant.

Third-party funding could be groundbreaking for the materialisation of consumer access to justice. As noted above, one of the most significant problems faced by consumer organisations and foundations in Poland is the lack of adequate funds for their operations. Undoubtedly, collective actions are very costly, and funding is a key factor in the success of group proceedings. Without proper funding, it is uncertain whether any consumer organisation in Poland would be interested in applying for registration as qualified entities entitled to bring representative action. Although third-party funding may address this issue, the following demonstrates that pursuing this option in practice might be challenging.

According to the Act amending the Act on Group Proceedings, third-party funding is subject to extensive oversight by both the court and the President of UOKiK, who supervises the entire system of representative entities. It seems questionable whether, under the new law, the defendant can challenge the source of funding of the representative entity at every stage of the proceedings. Practice indicates that if the defendant has the right to contest the claim, they will undoubtedly exercise that right, regardless of justification. It can be reasonably anticipated that this right will be utilised by the trader to prolong the duration of proceedings, which in general tend to be very lengthy. Consequently, at each stage of the proceedings, the court may reject the claim if it has reasonable concerns regarding the source of funding for the representative entity. At the court's request, the representative entity is required to disclose the source of funding for its general activities and provide proof of the funding source for specific representative actions. If the court determines that another entity influences the appropriate protection of consumer interests affecting the group proceeding pending before it, it must oblige the representative entity to refuse, reimburse, or change the funding source under pain of rejection of the claim. In this event, the court sends excerpts of the decision to the President of UOKiK, who will verify whether the representative entity meets the requirement for financial independence and remove it from the register. Consumers impacted by this decision can join other group proceedings or pursue their claims individually.

3.6 Conclusion

This chapter, with its evidence-based nature, aimed to examine the system of consumer collective redress in Poland. It can be assumed that almost 15 years of group proceedings have given Poland ample experience to evaluate how this mechanism operates. However, it has been found that although the number of claims submitted to the courts appears promising, only a few cases reached the final phase of proceedings where the court decided on the merits.

Moreover, this study revealed that the cases documented in the statistics from the Ministry of Justice do not accurately reflect the reality of collective redress in Poland. The number of collective claims does not correspond with the number of cases initiated. It became apparent that, although counted separately, many court files pertained to the same case. This discrepancy arose because collective claims were rejected because of formal deficiencies. After rectifying these formal issues—likely including the payment of court fees—the collective claims were refiled in the same court but assigned new file numbers. Some collective claims were initially rejected by the court for failing to meet the formal requirements for group proceedings. Since court decisions could be appealed, the second instance court later admitted these claims to the group proceedings. In such instances, the claims were refiled and, once more, assigned new file numbers. A similar situation occurred when proceedings were stayed after the commencement date (for instance, due to the defendant's bankruptcy). If a claim was resubmitted, it also received a new court file number. For sure, the sole analysis of the statistics of Ministry of Justice does not give a full picture of Polish collective redress system.

The examination of case law shows that the success of collective redress is closely linked to the subject matter of the claim. Some specific consumer claims are well suited for group proceedings, while others are likely better pursued through individual proceedings. It appears that small claims, such as those related to improper performance of travel package contracts or other forms of entertainment, are worth considering for group proceedings. The key to success lies in the common factual basis—the amount paid by consumers as a ticket price or holiday package. However, practice indicates that even such seemingly straightforward claims can take several years to resolve in group proceedings. In the case of low-value claims amounting to only several hundred PLN, consumers must be extremely persistent and determined in seeking redress if they are willing to wait so long for recovery.

Lengthy, multi-stage proceedings incur higher legal costs. Even if the group is represented by the municipal consumer ombudsman and there are no court fees, there are still costs associated with legal representation, which is compulsory in group proceedings. It is unrealistic to expect that legal attorneys will offer their services *pro bono*. Therefore, consumers will certainly think twice and weigh the potential benefits before going to court. The undeniable advantage of pursuing consumer claims in groups, rather than individually, is the absence of court fees when represented by a municipal consumer ombudsman, the Financial Ombudsman, or a representative entity within the meaning of RAD.

Another observation can be made based on analysis of collective claims brought in Poland against various insurers that charge so-called liquidation fees for policy termination (*polisolokaty*). All of these claims were either adjudicated in favour of the claimant or settled, whether in court or out of it.[102] It is important to note that in these cases, the contractual provisions were deemed abusive and were recorded in the register of prohibited clauses by the Court of Competition and Consumer Protection (SOKiK). This undoubtedly provided significant assistance to the court adjudicating the group proceedings concerning redress measures. Identifying a clause as abusive serves as a clear indication for a court ruling on follow-up actions that the claims related to the use of such a clause are valid.

Unfortunately, practice shows that this is not always the case. A prominent example is the case against Bank Millennium concerning loan agreements indexed to foreign currency.[103] The claimant argued that each member of the group had entered into an agreement based on the same abusive indexation clause, which was confirmed by a judgment of SOKiK and subsequently entered into the register of abusive clauses. Nonetheless, the court of first instance denied the collective claim. This is particularly surprising considering that the vast majority of similar claims brought in individual proceedings against the same bank are adjudicated in favour of consumers. It is also noteworthy that the claim was supported by the Commissioner for Human Rights and the Financial Ombudsman. There are no reasons, other than the judges' reluctance, that could reasonably justify why this claim was denied by the court of first instance.[104]

This leads me to the next observation that the judges' attitudes toward group proceedings are crucial for the effective enforcement of collective claims. A prime example is the case against the State Treasury concerning the Amber Gold scandal.[105] The proceedings were highly complex and involved intricate evidence. The court promptly ordered all procedural steps and although the proceedings lasted several years, their duration seems justified given the complexity of the case.

What is the reason for the different attitudes of the judges? The reluctance could be justified by the fact that, for the purpose of court statistics, group proceedings, which are generally more complex and involve a greater workload for the judges handling such cases, are counted the same as individual proceedings. This lack of differentiation in the allocation of cases makes some

102 Proceedings pending before the District Court in Warsaw in cases: file no. II C 222/16 '*AXA*'; file no. XXIV C 554/14 '*Generali*'; file no. III C 62/14 '*Skandia*'; file no. XXIV C 500/14 '*Skandia*'; file no. III C 1322/13 '*Aegon*'; file no. XXIV C 709/15 '*TU na Życie Europa*'; file no. I C 464/16 '*TU na Życie Europa*'.

103 Proceedings pending before the District Court in Warsaw in case: I C 1281/15 '*Bank Millennium*'.

104 Mucha (2024a: 105).

105 Proceedings pending before the District Court in Warsaw in case: XXV C 1614/16 '*Liability of the State Treasury for Amber Gold*'.

judges unwilling to adjudicate claims for group proceedings. Further, given the small number of group proceedings compared to individual cases, it is not surprising that judges tend to be reluctant towards relatively unknown group actions. Statistically, the average judge working in one of the 47 district courts in Poland will never adjudicate a collective claim or may only handle one such case during their professional career. A proposed solution to this issue is to establish a single court designated solely for group proceedings. This would enable judges to specialise in this type of litigation, share experiences and build consistent, nationwide case law, which in turn would help consumers and their representatives evaluate their chances for future collective claims. It is worth noting that in response to the nationwide crisis related to loan agreements in foreign currency, a specialised court for these claims was created, and its activities have been assessed very positively.

Would the situation for consumers pursuing collective claims in Poland improve with the implementation of RAD? There are some promising solutions relating to consumer representative actions that could slightly influence the number of consumer representative actions, with the most prominent one allowing for claims to be based on the same or a similar legal basis (as an alternative to the same or a similar factual basis). However, the system of group proceedings, including consumer claims, existed before, and the implementation of RAD did not bring any revolutionary reforms to the existing scheme. Not only do some old problems of group proceedings remain unsolved, but also some new issues have arisen. Two obstacles that I consider the most problematic are the chaotic structure of the consumer law enforcement system and the risk of the ineffectiveness of representative actions in practice.

The first issue concerns the complicated structure of law enforcement. Consumers, whose collective interests have been infringed, have several options for law enforcement. First, they can notify the President of UOKiK, who, although not required, may initiate administrative proceedings against the trader, resulting in a decision on injunctions in which the authority can determine public compensation. Alternatively, consumers may reach out to a representative entity (a consumer organisation or public authority registered by the President of UOKiK) that will file a representative action and commence group proceedings in court, seeking injunctive and/or compensatory measures. Lastly, for all other matters related to consumer claims, consumers can initiate group proceedings based on the 'old version' of the Act on Group Proceedings, which states, among other things, that a group member can initiate group proceedings on behalf of the group. This entire range of tools could be advantageous if consumers had knowledge about the specific instruments they could use and understood the consequences and potential interdependence of different proceedings. However, it is quite doubtful that the average consumer will comprehend this and choose an appropriate option to pursue their claim.

Additionally, the previously mentioned enforcement structure is vague due to the dual authority of the President of UOKiK operating on two enforcement paths. On the one hand, this authority can initiate administrative proceedings *ex officio* to seek injunctions, while on the other, it oversees the system of representative actions in such a way that it is responsible for the registration and monitoring of representative entities. Furthermore, it is quite confusing that actions for injunctions may be initiated either by the President of UOKiK or by representative entities; however, the authority will have clear priority in this matter. Before starting the group action seeking the injunctive measure, the representative entity must inform the President of UOKiK about it and must wait for the reply of the authority (from one to three months), which additionally slows down the proceedings. This renders the one-stop-shop actions, which could address the issue of ineffective procedures, entirely pointless.

This brings me to the second main concern discussed here: the effectiveness of representative actions. It is particularly controversial that representative actions are initiated in group proceedings, which are often lengthy, costly and risky. Polish judges interpret the requirements for certifying claims very strictly and many collective claims are rejected because they do not meet the criteria established for group proceedings. The case law concerning foreign currency loan agreements illustrates that it is often more advantageous to pursue claims individually rather than collectively.

RAD emphasises the role of consumer organisations as representative entities. However, it is highly questionable whether these organisations in Poland will be interested in applying for the status of representative entities. The primary issue faced by consumer organisations is the lack of adequate funding, which is particularly evident considering the high costs associated with group proceedings. The President of UOKiK identified 19 consumer organisations in Poland that could be, at least theoretically, interested in being recognised as representative entities. The authority assumes that each of these entities will initiate one collective action per year, which, in my opinion, is far too optimistic, given that no additional operational funds for consumer organisations have been allocated in the state budget. Furthermore, it has been shown that filing a collective claim in a Polish court does not guarantee the initiation of group proceedings, as many collective claims are returned or rejected as inadmissible for such actions. It is also possible, at least in theory, that representative actions will be initiated by entities recognised in other Member States; however, this scenario seems very unlikely at present.

Considering the obvious financial problems faced by consumer organisations in Poland, it is surprising that the Act amending the Act on Group Proceedings designates only one public authority authorised to file representative actions *ex lege*—namely, the Financial Ombudsman. It is predicted (again, perhaps too optimistically) that this authority will submit between six and eight representative actions per year. It is quite surprising that apart from the Financial Ombudsman, the new law does not recognise municipal consumer ombudsmen as representative entities. My research indicates that these institutions, operating at the regional level, provide genuine support for consumers by filing collective claims on their behalf.

Revising the research hypothesis from the book's introduction: the collective redress mechanism in Poland fails to ensure effective enforcement of consumer rights and a high standard of consumer protextion. This failure is not rooted in the legislative framework, which, despite a few noted shortcomings, is generally viewed favourably by practitioners and judges. The problem does not lie in the text of the law but rather in its practical application, and it is highly doubtful that the implementation of RAD will bring about significant change. A second-year law student understands that even the best transposition of the directive into national law is merely the initial step for its full implementation. To meet the objectives outlined in RAD, broad application and enforcement of transposed provisions are essential. For this to happen, some very basic conditions, being of great practical relevance, must be satisfied.

First, judges need to be trained on handling multi-stage group proceedings, as this could positively influence their attitudes towards such adjudications. Establishing a dedicated department for group proceedings would enhance the system's effectiveness, allowing judges to specialize in this type of procedure. Such a department could be set up within the District Court in Warsaw, where most group proceedings in Poland are currently taking place. It has been proved already, based on the experience of the Swiss franc loan department of the District Court in Warsaw, that this solution works in practice.

Further, creating a transparemt, easily accessible register of group proceedings is essential. Not only group representatives but (also potencial) group members shall have access to information about pending or concluded cases, allowing them to assess their chances of bringing or joining representative actions. It is alarming that currently, the majority of court decisions and judgmenets issued in group proceedings are not publised online, and the only way to obtain infromation about these cases is to request public information from the relevant court. By no means is information published nowadays by courts handling group proceedings to be conisdered adequate to serve a purpuse of register of cases.

Finally, representative entities must receive funding to effectively fulfill their roles. It is concerning that the rationale behind the Act amending the Act on Group Proceedings suggests no additional state budget funds are necessary for representative actions. The expectation is that there will only be a minor increase in the number of additional cases submitted to Polish courts. Such an assumption makes the entire concept of effective consumer law enforcement doomed to fail. If this narrative does not change, the only option left will be third-party funding. Alternatively, public enforcement of consumer collective interests could serve as a solution. This is undoubtedly a highly promising area that warrants further research.

References

Asłanowicz M (2018) *Ustawa o dochodzeniu roszczeń w postępowaniu grupowym. Komentarz*, Legalis, CH Beck (electronic source).

Faure M Weber F (2017) The diversity of the EU approach to law enforcement- towards a coherent model inspired by a law and economics approach, *German Law Review*, Vol. 18(4), pp. 823–880.

Jagielska M (2019) Collective redress and consumer enforcement in Poland: Why doesn't it work? In: Simon R, Muellerowa H (eds), *Efficient collective redress mechanisms in Visegrad 4 countries: An achievable target?*, Institute of State and Law of Czech Academy of Science, pp. 32–41.

Jurkowska-Zeidler A (2018) Aktualne problemy ochrony klienta na rynku bankowym z perspektywy działalności rzecznika finansowego, *Gdańskie Studia Prawnicze*, Vol. 39, pp. 29–44.

Kohutek K (2019) Rekompensata publiczna jako środek usunięcia skutków naruszenia zbiorowych interesów konsumentów: wątpliwości systemowo-kompetencyjne, *Studia Prawnicze. Rozprawy i Materiały*, Vol. 1(24), pp. 35–59.

Laskowska-Kulisz A (2022) Postępowanie grupowe jako przykład pozakodeksowego sądowego postepowania cywilnego, *Gdańskie Studia Prawnicze*, Vol. 5(27), pp. 225–255.

Mucha J (2019) Nowy model ochrony zbiorowych interesów konsumentów w UE i możliwości jego wdrożenia w Polsce, *Internetowy Kwartalnik Antymonopolowy i Regulacyjny*, Vol. 8(8), pp. 7–24.

Mucha J (2021) Public enforcement of consumer law in Poland: Mission impossible? *Krytyka Prawa,* Vol. 13(6), pp. 29–44.

Mucha J (2024a) From recipe to reality: The Polish way of collective redress, *Era Forum*, Springer, Vol. 25, pp. 97–108.

Mucha J (2024b) Sipping the enforcement cocktail: Poland's misadventures in implementing the representative actions directive, *Revue européenne de droit de la consummation*, Vol. 2, pp. 331–345.

Mucha J (2025) Protection of the financial consumers in the EU against unfair contract terms in the foreign currency loans, In: Damar-Blanken D, Kelly Louw M (eds), *Financial inclusion law, credit fairness and over-indebtedness*, Routledge 2025, pp.13-26.

Nekrosius V, Flaga-Gieruszyńska K (2021) The class action in Lithuania and Poland: History, experiences and lessons, *Review of Central and East European Law*, Vol. 46, pp. 234–264.

Okońska P (2024) Finansowanie sporów sądowych przez podmiot trzeci- perspektywa polska, *Internetowy Kwartalnik Antymonopolowy i Regulacyjny*, Vol. 13(1), pp. 47–62.

Piszcz A (2017) Compensatory collective redress: Will it be part of private enforcement of competition law in CEE countries?, *Yearbook of Antitrust and Regulatory Studies*, Vol. 10(15), pp. 223–250.

Pluskwa- Dąbrowski K (2019) Collective redress in consumer cases: How to launch in practice in Poland, In: Simon R, Mullerowa H (eds), *Efficient collective redress mechanisms in visegrad 4 countries: An achievable target?* Institute of State and Law of Czech Academy of Science, Prague, pp.129–136.

Rejdak M (2019) *Obowiązywanie w polskim porządku prawnym postępowania grupowego (ocena i perspektywa zmian)*, Wydawnictwo IWS.

Sieradzka M (2018) *Ustawa o dochodzeniu roszczeń w postępowaniu grupowym. Komentarz*. Wyd. 3, Wolters Kluwer.

Studzińska J (2016) Protecting the interests of the group (collective) in the jurisdiction of courts of common pleas and the Supreme Court in Poland, *Krytyka Prawa*, Vol. 8(3), pp. 162–168.

Tulibacka M (2018) Poland, In: Hodges C, Voet S (eds), *Delivering collective redress: New technologies*, Hart, pp. 128–151.

Tulibacka M (2024) Consumer justice: Do European know something we do not? *Emory International Law Journal*, Vol. 38(4), pp. 715–749.

Trzaska A (2019) Poland, In: Sanger C (ed), *The class action law review*, Law Business Research Ltd., pp. 155–169.

Trzaska- Śmieszek A, Osmęda M (2024) *Uprzywilejowany Rzecznik Finansowy*, Rzeczpospolita, 3 August 2024 (electronic source)

Annex no. 1: List of case files for group proceedings pending and/or closed between 01.01.2013-30.06.2020 before the District Court in Warsaw

WYKAZ SYGNATUR POSTEPOWAN GRUPOWYCH W TOKU I ZAKONCZONYCH OKRES 01-01-2013-30-06-2020

SYGNATURA SPRAWY	SPRAWA WTOKU	SPRAWA ZAKONCZONA	SPRAWA ZWR6CONA
I C 599/14		X	
I C 691/14		X	
I C 1385/14		X	
I C 566/15			X
I C 868/15		X	
I C 1281/15	26/10/2020		
I C 464/16	X		
I C 1235/19	X		
I C 916/20	**X**		
I C 771/13		X	
I C 1055/13			X
I C 1129/13		X	
I C 257/14		X	
I C 369/14			X
I C 172/15		X	
I C 269/15		X	
I C 414/15			X
I C 693/15			X
I C 695/15			X
I C 222/16	26/11/2020		
I C 423/16		X	
I C 570/19		X	
I C 902/20			X
III C 376/13		X	
III C 1024/13		X	
III C 1322/13		X	
III C 1391/13		X	
III C 62/14		X	
III C 881/14		X	

III C 55/15		X	
III C 56/15		X	
III C 328/15		X	
III C 603/15		X	
III C 798/15		X	
III C 1089/15		X	
III C 1122/15	X		
III C 171/16	X		
III C 1310/16		X	
III C 1316/20			X
IV C 96/13		X	
IV 448/14		X	
IV C 571/14		X	
IV 703/14		X	
IV C 269/16		X	
IV C 195/18	X		
IV C 281/18	X		
XXIV C 254/14		X	
XXIV C 269/14		X	
XXIV C 500/14		X	
XXIV C 554/14		X	
XXIV C 704/14			X
XXIV C 811/14		X	
XXIV C 1166/14		X	
XXIV C 1359/14		X	
XXIV C 339/15		X	
XXIV C 709/15	X		
XXIV C 109/16	21/09/2020		
XXIV C 736/16		X	
XXIV C 167/17		X	
XXIV C 191/17		X	
XXIV C 934/17		X	
XXIV C 540/20	X		

XXV C 148/14		X	
XXV C 358/14		X	
XXV 530/14		X	
XXV C 531/14		X	
XXV C 318/15		X	
XXV C 711/15		X	
XXV C 918/15		X	
XXV C 1529/15	X		
XXV C 308/16	X		
XXV C 1078/16		X	
XXV C 1556/16			X
XXV C 1614/16	X		
XXV C 843/17	X		
XXV C 250/18		X	
XXV C 461/18	X		
XXV C 1106/18	X		
XXV C 2227/20	6/10/2020		
XXV C 2239/20	X		

Index

Note: Page numbers in **bold** reference tables and 'n' denotes reference footnotes

abusive litigation 14
Act amending the Act on Group Proceedings (Poland) 102–103, 114; President of UOKiK 108; recognition of representative entities 106; third-party funding 109–110
Action Plan of European Commission (1996) 15
Act of 16 February 2007 on Competition and Consumer Protection (ACCP) (Poland) 102
Act on Court Costs in Civil Cases (Poland) 102, 106–107
Act on Group Proceedings (Poland) 80–81, 112–113; amendments to 102; Financial Ombudsman 97–100; legislative framework on group proceedings 81–83; liberalisation of certification requirements 104–105; Municipal Consumer Ombudsman 96–97; register of group proceedings 84–86
Act on Pursuing Claims in Group Proceedings (Poland) 4, 107
Act on the Resolution of Mass Claims in Collective Actions (WAMCA) (2020) (Netherlands) 57, 62–68, 74–75; *Evolve Media* case 66–67; *Oracle* case 67–68; *Volkswagen* case 65–66
Action Plan of European Commission (1996) 15
ad hoc designation of representative entities 37
admissibility of collective actions (Belgium) 50–51
Ageas (Fortis) case (the Netherlands) 61–62
American class action style 9; *vs.* EU collective redress 10–15
Apple case (Belgium) 57
autonomy: of parties regarding group composition 14 RAD 34–35

Belgian Consumer Mediation Service 52
Belgian Ministry of Economic Affairs 51
Belgium 48–49, 73–74; admissibility 50–51; Belgian Code of Economic Law (CEL) 49–52; class action process 50–51; compulsory negotiation phase 51; Consumer Mediation Service 52; Consumer Ombudsman Service 50, 54–55; Energy Ombudsman 54–55; opt-in system 49, 51; pay-outs 52; settlement impasse 51–52; standing 50

breach: of competition law 16; of consumer law 23
business concerns, Proposal for RAD 29–32

C-119/15 *Partner*, Court of Justice of the European Union 3, 22
C-195/17 *Krüsemann*, Court of Justice of the European Union 56
C-319/20 *Meta*, Court of Justice of the European Union 3–4
C-472/10 *Invitel*, Court of Justice of the European Union 3, 21
C-498/16 *Schrems*, Court of Justice of the European Union 38-39
Cambridge Analytica scandal (Belgium) 53–54
case file no. I C 464/16-, 'TU Życie Europa I', District Court in Warsaw 101
case file no. I C 599/14–'OFE,' District Court in Warsaw 87–88
case file no. I C 1281/15–'Bank Millenium,' District Court in Warsaw 88–90
case file no. II C 222/16–'AXA,' District Court in Warsaw 93–94
case file no. II C 771/13–'Travel agency Gromada,' District Court in Warsaw 93
case file no. III C 376/13–'Spółdzielnia przy Metrze', District Court in Warsaw 90–91
case file no. III C 603/15–'Polski Związek Motorowy,' District Court in Warsaw 95
case file no. XXIV C 339/15–'Remuneration of the police civil servants,' District Court in Warsaw 91
case file no. XXIV C 554/14–'Generali,' District Court in Warsaw 94
case file no. XXIV C 709/15-'TU Życie EUROPA II', District Court in Warsaw 101
case file no. XXV C 250/18–'Bank BZWBK–Amber Gold pyramid scheme,' District Court in Warsaw 91–92
case file no. XXV C 315/15–'Home Brokers,' District Court in Warsaw 95–96
case file no. XXIV C 339/15–'Remuneration of the police civil servants,' District Court in Warsaw 91
case file no. XXV C 1614/16–'Liability of the State Treasure for Amber Gold,' District Court in Warsaw 94–95
CAT *see* Competition Appeal Tribunal
CEL *see* Code of Economic Law
certification requirements, Act on Group Proceedings (Poland) 104–105
challenges to Directive 2009/22/EC 18–24
civil cases, collective claims (Poland) **84**
Civil Procedure Rules (CRP) (England and Wales) 70
CJEU *see* Court of Justice of the European Union
class action process (Belgium) 50–51
Code of Economic Law (CEL) (Belgium) 49–52; *Apple* case 57; *energy suppliers* case 54–55; *Facebook-Cambridge Analytica* scandal (Belgium) 53–54; *Groupon* (*Luierbox*) case 53; *Ryanair* case 55–56
collective actions: Act on the Resolution of Mass Claims in Collective Actions (WAMCA) (2020) 62–68; numbers on (in Poland) 83–84
collective claims in civil courts (Poland) **84**
collective consumer interests 104
collective entities, limitations of 4

collective procedure for consumers in competition law (England and Wales) 72–73
collective redress framework within RAD, critical review of 34–41
collective settlements (Netherlands) 58–68
commercial litigation funders 41
Commissioner for Human Rights (Poland) 101–102
commonality requirement (Poland) 82
common principles for injunctive and compensatory collective redress mechanisms 16
commonality requirement (Poland) 82
compensation 24; Proposal for RAD 25–27; *see also* collective settlements
compensatory redress 16
compensatory relief 16–17
Competition Appeal Tribunal (CAT) (England and Wales) 72
competition law: breach of 16; collective procedure for consumers (England and Wales) 72–73
compulsory negotiation phase (Belgium) 51
consensus in the trilogue, Proposal for RAD 32–33
consumer collective redress framework 15–18
Consumer Forum (Poland) 102
consumer law, breach of 23
consumer law enforcement 47
Consumer Ombudsman Service (Belgium) 50, 54–55
consumer protection 2
continental law judges 42
contingency fees 11–12, 32, 83
Converium case (the Netherlands) 61
cost of proceedings 106–107; Directive 2009/22/EC 19–20; Proposal for RAD 26–27; RAD 40–41
Council of the European Union, Proposal for RAD 33
Court of Competition and Consumer Protection (SOKiK) (Poland) 111
Court of Justice of the European Union (CJEU) 3; C-119/15 *Partner* 3, 22; C-195/17 *Krüsemann* 56; C-319/20 *Meta* 3–4; C-472/10 *Invitel* 3, 21; *Invitel* 3, 21; *Meta* 3–4; *Schrems*, Maximilian 38–39; *Schrems* 38–39; *Schrems* judgment 38–39
cross-border actions, Directive 2009/22/EC 23–24
cross-border representative actions 33, 36–38; Proposal for RAD 28–29
CRP *see* Civil Procedure Rules
C-498/16 *Schrems*, Court of Justice of the European Union 38-39

DEJF *see* Diesel Emission Justice Foundation (the Netherlands)
denied cases, District Court in Warsaw 87–92
DG *see* directorate-generals (European Commission)
DG for Competition (European Commission) 16
DG for Health and Consumer Protection (European Commission) 16
DG *see* directorate-generals (European Commission)
Diesel Emission Justice Foundation (DEJF) (the Netherlands) 65–66
*Dieselgate case (*in England and Wales*)* 70–72
Dieselgate case (in the Netherlands) 65–66different classifications of collective redress 9
Directive 93/13/EEC of the Council of 5 April 1993 on unfair terms in consumer contracts 20–21, 102
Directive 98/27/EC of the European Parliament and of the Council of 19 May 1998 on injunctions

for the protection of consumers' interests 3, 15, 23
Directive 2009/22/EC of the European Parliament and of the Council of 23 April 2009 on injunctions for the protection of consumers' interests 9, 15, 24, 39, 43, 80; challenges to 18–24
Directive 2020/1828 on Representative Actions (RAD) 1, 5–6, 9, 17–18, 48, 113; cost of proceedings 40–41; critical review of collective redress framework 34–41; cross-border representative actions 36–38; domestic representative actions 36–38; funding qualified entities 40–41; implementing in Poland 102–110; limits of 34–35; opt-in/opt-out 35–36
directorate-generals (DG) 16
discovery 12
District Court's in Warsaw case law (group proceedings) 86–87; 'Axa Życie Towarzystwo Ubezpieczeń' 98; Amber Gold 91–92; AXA 99; case file no. I C 464/16 101; case file no. I C 599/14–'OFE' 87–88; case file no. I C 1281/15–'Bank Millenium' 88–90; case file no. II C 222/16–'AXA' 93–94; case file no. II C 771/13–'Travel agency Gromada' 93; case file no. III C 376/13–'Spółdzielnia przy Metrze' 90–91; case file no. III C 603/15–'Polski Związek Motorowy' 95; case file no. XXIV C 339/15–'Remuneration of the police civil servants' 91; case file no. XXIV C 554/14–'Generali' 94; case file no. XXIV C 554/14 94; case file no. XXIV C 709/15 101; case file no. XXV C 250/18–'Bank BZWBK–Amber Gold pyramid scheme' 91–92; case file no. XXV C 315/15–'Home Brokers' 95–96; case file no. XXV C 1614/16–'Liability of the State Treasure for Amber Gold' 94–95; Home Brokers, case file no. XXV C 315/15–'Home Brokers' 95–96; Generali 99–100; 'Travel agency Gromada' 93; TU Życie Europa 101
domestic representative actions 36–38
duration of proceedings, Proposal for RAD 27
Dutch Collective Settlement Act (2005) (WCAM) 57; *Ageas* (Fortis) case 61–62; collective settlements 58–62; *Converium* case 61; *DES* case 60

EC-React 42
EEA *see* European Commission
Energy Ombudsman (Belgium) 54–55
energy suppliers case (Belgium) 54–55
enforcement mechanisms 7
enforcement of consumer law 47
England and Wales 68–69, 75–76; collective procedure for consumers in competition law 72–73; group litigation order (GLO) 69–72
EOKM Foundation (the Netherlands) 67; *see also* the *Evolve Media* case (the Netherlands)
EU Charter of Fundamental Rights 68
EU consumer policy 2
European Commission 15; Action Plan (1996) 15; EC-React 42; A New Deal for Consumers 17
European Economic Area (EEA) 50
European ombudsman for cross-border representative actions, establishment of 37–38
European Union, collective redress *vs.* US class action 10–15
Evolve Media case (the Netherlands) 66–67

Facebook-Cambridge Analytica scandal (Belgium) 53–54; *see also Facebook* case
Financial Ombudsman (Poland) 82, 96–100, 105–107
foreign currency loan crisis (Poland) 101–102
Fortis case (the Netherlands) 61–62
funding: collective redress 41–42; qualified entities, RAD 26–27, 40–41; third-party funding, 109–110

General Data Protection Regulation (GDPR) 68
globalisation 1–2
GLO *see* group litigation order (GLO)
globalisation 1–2
group actions 9
group formation in group proceedings (Poland) 82–83
group litigation, duration of proceedings 28
group litigation order (GLO), England and Wales 69–72, 75
group proceedings (Poland): costs of 106–107; before District Court in Warsaw 86–96; RAD 104; register of 84–86
group settlements 10

Hungary, national consumer protection authority (NFH) 21; *see also* C-472/10 *Invitel*
infringement of consumer rights 7
injunctions: Directive 2009/22/EC 18–19; Proposal for RAD 25–26
injunctive relief 16–17
insignificant loss 25
Insurance Ombudsman *see* Financial Ombudsman (Poland)
international jurisdiction 38

judges, attitudes toward group proceedings 111–112

lack of private international law rules for representative actions 38–39
lawyers, hourly fees 11–12
legal costs, Proposal for RAD 26–27
legal remedies, Directive 2009/22/EC 18–19
legislative framework 48; for collective redress (Poland) 81–83
liberalisation of certification requirements, Act on Group Proceedings (Poland) 104–105
limitations of collective entities 4
limiting collective redress process 31n124
litigation boom 14
loser pays principle 19–20, 30
Luierbox case (Belgium) 53

mass harm, Proposal for RAD 25
mass litigation 9
mediation (Belgium) 52
Merricks v. Mastercard (England and Wales)72–73
missing criteria for qualified entities, Proposal for RAD 30–31
model/test case 9
municipal consumer ombudsman (Poland) 82, 88, 96–97, 105
My Data Is Mine campaign (Belgium) 53; *see also Facebook* case
My Diesel Claim (England and Wales) 72; *see also Dieselgate* case study

national consumer protection authority (NFH) (Hungary) 21
Netherlands 57–58, 74–75; Act on the Resolution of Mass Claims in Collective Actions (WAMCA) (2020) 62–68; Dutch Collective Settlement Act (2005) 58–62
A New Deal for Consumers 17
non-discrimination, RAD 35

Office of Competition and Consumer Protection (UOKiK) (Poland) 22, 80; President of

UOKiK 100–101, 103, 105–107, 112–113; role of President 80–81
opt-in system 13–14, 33; Belgium 49, 51, 74; group litigation order (GLO) (England and Wales) 70; RAD 35–36
opt-out system 32–33; *Apple* case 56–57; Belgium 74; RAD 35–36; US class action 12–14
Oracle case (Netherlands) 67–68

pay-out phase of class action (Belgium) 52
Poland: Act amending the Act on Group Proceedings 102–103, 108–110, 114; Act of 16 February 2007 on Competition and Consumer Protection (ACCP) 102; Act of 28 July 2005 on Court Costs in Civil Cases 102; Act on Court Costs in Civil Cases 106–107; Act on Pursuing Claims in Group Proceedings *see* Act on Group Proceedings; Commissioner for Human Rights 101–102; contingency fees 83; costs of group proceedings 106–107; Financial Ombudsman 82, 96–100; group formation 82–83; group proceedings before District Court in Warsaw 86–96; implementation of RAD 102–110; legislative framework for collective redress 81–83; municipal consumer ombudsman 82, 96–97; numbers on collective action 83–84; Office of Competition and Consumer Protection (UOKiK) 22, 80–81, 100–101, 103, 105–107, 112–113; register of group proceedings 84–86; third-party funding 109–110; *see also* District Court in Warsaw
President of UOKiK 100–101, 103, 105–108, 112–113
Privacy Collective Foundation (the Netherlands) 67–68
private enforcement 9; Belgium 48–57; England and Wales 68–73; Netherlands 57–68
procedural autonomy, RAD 34–35
Proposal for a Directive on Competition Damages of 2013 16
Proposal for the Representative Actions Directive (RAD) 9, 17–18, 24–25; business concerns 29–32; consensus in the trilogue 32–33; cross-border representative actions 28–29; duration of proceedings 27; final effect of the decision 27–28; injunctions 25–26; legal costs and funding qualified entities 26–27
Proposal for the Directive on Collective Actions 16
Proposal for the Representative Actions Directive *see* Proposal for RAD
public enforcement of collective consumer interests 80
punitive damages 11, 32; Proposal for RAD 30

RAD *see* Directive 2020/1828 on Representative Actions
recognition of representative entities, RAD 105–106
Recommendation 2013/396/EU 17, 24, 28, 43
register of group proceedings (Poland) 84–86
Regulation (EU) No 2016/679 of the European Parliament and Council of 27 April 2016 on the protection of natural persons with regard to the processing of personal data and on the free movement of such data, and repealing Directive 95/46/EC 68n83
Regulation No 44/2001 of the Council of 22 December 2000 on jurisdiction and the recognition

and enforcement of judgements in n civil and commercial matters 38–39
Regulation No 261/2004 of the European Parliament and of the Council of 11 February 2004 establishing common rules on compensation and assistance to passengers in the event of denied boarding and of cancellation or long delay of flights 56
Regulation No 1215/2012 of the European Parliament and of the Council of 12 December 2012 on jurisdiction and the recognition and enforcement of judgments in civil and commercial matters 38
representative actions 1, 9–10, 42; compensation 25; cross-border representative actions 28–29; England and Wales 69–72; lack of private international law rules 38–39
Representative Actions Directive (RAD) 9, 80
representative entities 113; recognition of (Poland) 105–106
risk of abusive litigation, Proposal for RAD 29–30
routes to consumer collective redress framework 15–18
Ryanair case (Belgium) 55–56

settlement impasse (Belgium) 51–52
small and medium-sized enterprises (SMEs) 49–50
SOKiK *see* Court of Competition and Consumer Protection (Poland)
standardisation requirements, Act on Group Proceedings (Poland) 105
standing for qualified entities (Belgium) 50
Stop Online Shaming (Netherlands) 67

Testachats (Belgium) 53–57
third-party funding (Poland) 40–42, 109–110; Proposal for RAD 26–27, 31–33; RAD 35

unfair contract terms 21–23
UOKiK *see* Office of Competition and Consumer Protection (Poland)
US class action 9, 30; *vs. EU* collective redress 10–15
US Federal Rules of Civil Procedure, discovery 12

Volkswagen case (Dieselgate), England and Wales 70–72
Volkswagen case (Dieselgate), the Netherlands 65–66
Volkswagen case (Dieselgate), England and Wales 70–72

Wales *see* England and Wales
WAMCA *see* Act on the Resolution of Mass Claims in Collective Actions (2020)
WCAM *see* Dutch Collective Settlement Act (2005)

Zurich Financial Securities (ZFS) 61; *see also Converium* case (the Netherlands)

For Product Safety Concerns and Information please contact our EU representative GPSR@taylorandfrancis.com Taylor & Francis Verlag GmbH, Kaufingerstraße 24, 80331 München, Germany

Printed and bound by CPI Group (UK) Ltd, Croydon, CR0 4YY
14/09/2026
02216243-0012